SHOWJUMPING

SHOWJUMPING

Preparation, Training and Competition

JOHN SMART

Howell Book House Inc.
230 Park Avenue, New York, N.Y. 10169

First published in Great Britain in 1987 by
The Crowood Press

**Published 1987 by Howell Book House Inc.
230 Park Avenue, New York, N.Y. 10169**

Library of Congress Cataloging-in-Publication Data

Smart, John, 1942-
  Showjumping.

  Bibliography: p.
  Includes index.
  1. Show jumping. I. Title. II. Title: Show jumping.
SF295.5.S63 1987   798.2′5   87-3728
ISBN 0-87605-868-3

Acknowledgements

Photographs by Kit Houghton and Gay O'Gorman

Thanks to Diana Tidd for typing, and special thanks to Malcolm Severs for all his help.

Typeset by Alacrity Phototypesetters, Weston-super-Mare
Printed in Great Britain at the University Printing House, Oxford

Contents

	Introduction	7
1	Flat Work	12
2	Basic Jumping	38
3	Related Distances	68
4	Approaching Advanced Jumping	79
5	Lungeing	90
6	At the Show	97
7	Bits and Bitting	104
8	The Use and Abuse of Gadgets	111
9	Horse Fitness and Welfare	119
	Conversions	122
	Useful Addresses	123
	Further Reading	124
	Index	125

Introduction

Training

Aims

No matter what equestrian discipline you follow, the better you ride, the more readily the horse understands what you are trying to make him do and the easier it is for him to comply with your wishes. Every moment spent working and improving your horse will improve your riding technique – but, with the best will in the world, the horse can only go as well as you can ride him. During training you will both learn continuously, and it is worth remembering that what you learn on one horse will be useful when you ride another. After all, a riding career is rarely limited to just one horse.

All horses can jump but some have a greater ability to take to the air than others. To discover and develop this ability, you need to be trained yourself. However, you will never be able to make a horse give what he does not have to give; any jumping horse must have the basic ability from the word go. Training will not make him jump higher, but exercises will improve his technique and make it less physically demanding for him, enabling you to make maximum use of his innate ability.

The horse's athletic ability to jump fences may not always be enough, since you have to be able to make use of it. Therefore, half the reason for training is to enable you to ride to the right place at the right time, and in the right frame of mind. Only then can the horse make full use of whatever natural talent he has.

One of the reasons we do physical exercises is in order to influence the horse mentally, so that our performance will conform to what other people consider 'normal'. Whether we are doing a dressage test or jumping around a course of fences, horse and rider, as a partnership, must come to terms with whatever pattern the course builder has laid out. The course designer does not make allowances for individual horses and riders, and on every occasion we have to be able to adapt to whatever he produces. He lays out his course, we adjust to fit the pattern.

Approach

Jumping a course of fences is, as much as anything, a test of how well you are progressing with your training. However, you don't need to jump fences to correct faults or perfect technique. I like to get the basics right by putting problems into departments: fast horses need to be slowed down, slow ones speeded up, long horses need rounding up and short horses need to be lengthened. There is no art in being able to go long *or* short: the art is in being able to do either, depending upon the demands of the course builder.

In simple terms, then, riding a course of fences is a series of lengthened and shortened strides. If these changes cannot be done easily in trot or canter on the flat, they will be that much more difficult under the stress of competition, so what is needed first is a general routine.

I like to make the horse calm and relaxed, and then introduce exercises to warm him and loosen him up, while keeping him attentive and obedient to my signals. As he begins to listen, I can gradually make him work harder. Naturally there will be variations in this approach, as no two horses are the same. It is the job of the rider to identify the idiosyncracies and difficulties of each horse and to correct them during the exercises.

If the horse is not responding to the leg or the hand I will introduce exercises that can correct or improve these faults. At the same time, I try to make the work interesting and varied – a mixture of perfecting what the horse already knows and teaching something new. Some of these exercises can be on a loose rein because when a horse has shown he can go in a rounded outline for you it is not necessary for him to prove it all the time.

Training Factors

As this work progresses the horse will become stronger and fitter and he will be mentally and physically more capable of working for longer periods. However, the progress that you make will depend on several factors: your riding ability, the age and general well-being of the horse, the amount of time that you can devote to the horse's training and the facilities at your disposal.

Variation Ideally, during training, you and the horse will be on the same side – it shouldn't be a battle to train a horse. Horses can enjoy working, and if new movements are introduced at the right time, and in the correct manner, there will always be enough variation to keep you and the horse interested in what you are doing; neither of you should become bored. Bored horses tire quickly, start looking for evasions and try to get out of whatever it is that you want them to do. Only by constantly keeping the work and exercises varied and interesting can this be avoided – and it must be avoided if you want to get things right.

Horse welfare Whether I am riding or training I try to praise good points before criticising mistakes and I try to eliminate any pains that are stopping the horse from concentrating fully. An amazing number of people will complain about a horse shaking his head or evading the bit and, when you check his teeth, you find they are very sharp; sometimes the mouth is even ulcerated. These are very painful conditions and they make it virtually impossible for the horse to give his full concentration to his work. Similarly, badly fitting tack will work against you, so make every effort to sort out these physical problems before you attempt to overcome the mental ones. Horses need to be wormed, shod and have their teeth rasped at regular intervals and these jobs must be done correctly. Failure to do so will result in an unhappy and, in some cases, untrainable horse.

Communication The word 'dressage' is a French word and the literal translation in English is 'training'. So, no matter whether you call it ground work, flat work or dressage, what you are doing is training, rather than simply exercising, the horse. Everything you do will influence him and the aim must be to produce a horse that is both physically fit and mentally balanced. Even if you do not plan to compete in dressage competitions, the more correct you can make your movements in training, the clearer will be your communication with the horse and the more general benefit you will derive from them. After all, the 'correct' techniques are only correct because thousands of very talented trainers and riders over the years have shown that they achieve the best results. To get these results you must always have a clear picture in your mind of what it is that you want to achieve; every exercise must have a purpose and you must know precisely what that purpose is. The more positively you can give signals to the horse, the easier it is for him to understand what you intend and to comply with your wishes; I hope that the order in which I set out the exercises will show that one can lead into the other, almost as natural progressions.

Assessing progress Do not expect everything to be perfect all the time – especially with a young horse. Be satisfied as long as a progressive pattern is emerging. The main thing is not to measure progress day by day, or even week by week; at the end of each month, if you can say that you and your horse are a better partnership than you were the month before then obviously you are on the right lines. As long as you are taking three steps forward to every one backwards, you are making progress. Remember, too, that in training we do not test a horse's confidence, but rather build that confidence. In this context the odd mistake will not be the end of the world. In fact providing the blunders do not happen too often, the occasional mistake can be beneficial.

Riding systems You must never allow yourself to be put off by mistakes or to be influenced by people who say you are using the wrong 'system' of riding. There are many such systems – German, American, French, Italian, and others – but in fact they are all the same product with different packaging. An American horse is no less disciplined than a German horse: if the German horse is over-bent and 'pushed up together', and the American horse, perhaps with flowing mane and tail, is in a slightly longer outline, this does not mean that the American horse is any less disciplined or athletic than the German horse. The amount of international travel currently undertaken by top horses means that they all have to come out and jump courses anywhere, and they do not necessarily always win in their home country.

Approach to Jumping

Assessing Horse and Rider

When assessing a horse, never look at him in isolation, but in combination with his rider – assess them together as a pair. After all, the object of any training exercise is to get horse and rider working in partnership. As a trainer, I frequently sit on a horse to demonstrate a point or correct a fault, but this is in order to get some idea of the problems the rider is having, rather than for the rider to see how something is done. Unless I know the temperament of the horse, what sort of jumping ability he has, and his willingness, or otherwise, to work, I cannot really begin to put the two pieces of the jigsaw together. Often, for instance, a horse and rider will come out and consistently make the same mistakes; for me to tell whether the fault is with the horse or rider, I must mount and see what the horse does for me. Only when that is decided can I begin to sort out the particular problems of the combination.

Having said that, it is important to remember that consistent and regular work is required to get any horse and rider going well together. Walk, trot, canter and jumping must become integral aspects of everyday life. Horses must accept that this is the pattern of their work. It is no good having a horse who is quiet and obedient on the flat, but who becomes uncontrollable with excitement whenever he sees a jump. This will not happen if he has been trained to accept jumping as a natural part of his daily routine. The routine must be flexible, so that the horse cannot predict what you are going to do on any one day; by the same token, however, you must ensure that he practises all four basic elements of his training.

Rider's Work

It is equally important that you do not get over-excited when approaching a jump. This will transmit itself to the horse and he will come to regard jumping as something out of the ordinary, consequently becoming much harder to control. If you are excited by jumping, you must strive to be as matter of fact as possible when schooling over poles and jumps, so encouraging the horse to accept that jumping is simply part of the daily work. You must also learn to put jumping in a correct perspective. Remember that most of the work you do with any horse is flat work; when you are in the jumping arena you are unlikely to be there for more than 90 seconds. That is not long, and of those 90

seconds, 70 are spent on the flat getting from one jump to the next. Flat work is therefore the secret to successful show jumping. Unless you can achieve your riding aims on the flat, you will never achieve them in the air. If your horse ambles into trot three strides after the leg aid on the flat, he will not respond to the leg when you ask him the question as you approach a fairly large fence. Small mistakes on the flat magnify themselves into large jumping mistakes, so get the flat work right and the rest will take care of itself, to a great extent.

You must be capable of exercising total control over your horse's speed. In my experience a good 70 per cent of horses who stop at fences, started out by rushing at them. The rider approaching the fence appreciates the speed but leaves the decision on whether the fence is jumped or not to the horse. If the horse is going so fast that he has nothing left to offer, even with the rider's legs wrapped on tight, the rider gives up, attempts to steer and hopes for the best. This often results in the horse being so far off the fence, that he has to put in an emergency short stride which often leads to a stop.

If the horse you are riding is completely new to you, be cautious rather than aggressive; do not mount up and give the strange animal an almighty boot in the ribs. Many horses will take violent exception to this, and you could well end up on the floor. Even if the horse looks calm and placid, give him the benefit of the doubt and offer him the correct aid; apart from safety considerations, it is only by doing this that you can discover his faults.

Each horse and rider is a unique combination, with its own peculiar strengths and weaknesses. During training, you must strive to get the horse going in the direction, and at the pace, that you dictate. All trainers, instructors, coaches – whatever you like to call them – are looking for this end product. Their methods may vary but the aim is always the same.

In any training situation there are three personalities involved: the trainer, the rider and the horse. To get these three working together it may be necessary to 'bend' a few 'rules', which are, after all, just guide-lines; we all have to experiment a little as we go along. This book is simply based on the methods I have evolved to reach the desired end during my years as a trainer. If there is a theme in the book, it is that it is not what you do, but what you get from it that counts. Variety is more than the spice of life, it is the key to good riding.

1 Flat Work

Jumping around a course of fences basically involves a series of lengthened and shortened strides. If this is difficult for you to do in trot or canter on the flat, it will be much more difficult with the extra impulsion of jumping. A horse on his forehand, for instance, probably knocking down fences with his front legs, will not improve if you simply continue to jump fences in an attempt to cure the problem. You must take the horse back to basics.

Basic Revision Work

Lightening the Forehand

Start at the trot. Exercise and work the horse to lighten his forehand and get greater engagement from the hind quarters. Once achieved in trot, you will find that the canter will be so much better and, by the time you come to jump, the problem will have been resolved. If a horse is on his forehand in trot, he will be worse in canter and the speed of jumping will exaggerate the problem still further. Lightening the forehand by engaging the hind quarters, and making the horse carry himself correctly is the only cure.

This work is always best done at the trot. If you start off in working canter, you lengthen the horse to the fence so that he can open out as he jumps. On landing he has to be immediately rounded up, and this happens so fast that you will not be aware of whether you achieved your objective or not; far better to practise in trot so that you can be sure of getting what you ride for. When, eventually, it is time to repeat the exercise in canter, your horse will hopefully have already mastered the basic technique.

Lengthening and Shortening the Strides

Depending on the conformation and natural ability of your horse, there will be slight variations in the ease with which he performs the exercises. Before trying to lengthen a horse's trot, especially in a young or short-striding horse, ask him to slow his working trot and, once this is established, push him forward into working trot.

Slowing the working trot To slow the horse down, make a series of little checks with the fingers and consciously slow the rise to the trot. Try to keep your legs as close to the horse's side as possible without actually pushing him on.

The rein aids should always be light and frequent rather than long yanks. If the horse's head comes up when you check, you are checking him too hard. Ideally you should aim for a rhythm, and attempt to maintain that rhythm in the slower trot. Some young horses might find this difficult; they will try to speed up or fall back into a walk. Once the slower trot is established, let him get used to the rhythm before going forward again into working trot. Do this by

*Fig 1   A balanced, active working trot, showing a good outline,
although the rider is looking down.*

*Fig 2   The horse shows no resistance to light checks with the fingers
which make him a little more rounded in a slower trot.*

nudging with your legs – not a hard push against the horse's sides – until the more active trot is achieved, and concentrate on keeping the rhythm and outline as it was when you started.

Slowing the working trot is also useful for teaching young horses the signal to go from trot to walk. It is much easier for the horse to understand the aids, and he can respond that much more quickly, if he is working slowly. When walk is signalled from a slower trot the horse is in no doubt. Gradually you can increase the pace until the horse understands the walk signal in a full working trot. By adopting this patient approach, you will not be tempted to put your whole bodyweight on the reins to change down, and you will not invite the horse to lean into your hands.

Into medium trot Once you can feel the stride lengthening as you push up from slow trot to working trot, you will begin to feel more push from the hind quarters. This is the time to think about lengthening further into a medium trot. To do this, lower your hands a little to enable the horse to go slightly longer in his outline, while you maintain contact with both reins. Push him forward more purposefully with your legs, and try to

Fig 3   *The rider lowers his hands a little while giving the signal for the horse to lengthen. A good lengthening is shown.*

rise forward and down, rather than up and down. This is because you will have to be in the air longer, due to the increased stride, and rising forward allows you to use up that time without rising higher. This exercise should be done in rising trot, as it is much easier to maintain the constant rhythm. It helps, too, to begin lengthening the trotting stride quite soon after cantering. The horse has a reservoir of impulsion at this time – impulsion which is lacking if you ask him to lengthen after a loose-rein walk.

As the exercise develops and you are able to achieve a positive transition from one pace to another, ask the horse to

Fig 4 *Encouraging the horse to walk out by walking on a downward slope – the foot meets the ground having travelled slightly further on the slope than it would travel on the level.*

change up and down every six or seven strides, looking all the time to change stride with minimum alteration to the rhythm, outline and general picture of the horse.

It is easier to shorten a long-striding horse than it is to lengthen a short-striding one. Even so, if you concentrate on a gradual build-up, and get the horse to accept willingly the co-ordination of leg and hand, you can get him to resist his natural temptation to quicken and hurry his stride. It is a slow process and patience is needed, but success will come and, when it does, the horse will be fitter and stronger, and able to attempt the same exercise in canter.

The aim when cantering is to be able to lengthen and shorten on a straight line but, to start with, it is best to lengthen on the straight and shorten on a circle. If the horse is strong willed, headstrong, and persists in trying to have his own way, make him do the opposite of what he wants.

On the slower horse, make your signals quicker rather than stronger, almost to the point of startling him with your legs, and do short, sharp exercises that keep him guessing. The more excitable horse, on the other hand, needs long, slow exercises, with not too many changes. Try to start off slower than working trot, and gradually push him on as he begins to relax. Once you feel he is relaxing a little, make a few simple changes of direction while keeping the aids to a minimum. Talk to him all the time and pat him on the neck as much as you can, to reassure him. However, do not expect too much, too soon. Getting an excitable horse to relax is the most difficult part of his work and that initial breakthrough is often a long time coming. If you are patient and work systematically on all aspects of his work, the time will come when everything falls into place and you can see some tangible results for your efforts.

Reducing stiffness   One of the dangers in making corrections and adjustments is, of course, that you can often go too far the other way. Take a horse who is stiff and one-sided to the right, for instance. If you do exercises that soften his right side, he will eventually change sides and become stiff to the left; you may merely have reversed the problem. If, however, he is not as stiff to the left as he was to the right, he is nearer to being straight. A balanced approach is required that works the stiff side just that little bit more than the soft side. You must be sympathetic to the problems the horse is having, and understand his difficulties; do not expect to make chalk into cheese overnight. Go slowly and do not be disconcerted during the transition period, when the horse is neither what he was, nor what you want him to be be. There is always a slightly unsettled period in the middle of any training exercise, but perseverance usually wins the day.

Progressive Work

Reverse Half Volte

The reverse half volte is one of the best exercises to start you off in flat work – it is, after all, just the formal name for a turn on the forehand at the walk. If up to now your exercises have only been concerned with pushing the horse forward, it is not surprising that increased leg, to the horse, seems to be asking for more speed. Essentially the reverse half volte is a simple

Fig 5   The horse shows good movement off the leg. The front legs make a straightforward half circle, the hind legs make a larger half circle, with good crossing of the legs.

exercise to get the horse to move away from the pressure of a single leg. As an aid, you will need a straight line – preferably a fence, hedge or wall – because the aim is to get the horse to incline away from the straight track or wall at about 25 or 30 degrees. Once the horse has started the inclined line, keep it straight for about three metres and then make a half circle back to the track. The purpose of this is that the front legs make a straightforward half circle back to the straight line, while the back legs, in yielding to your leg, make a bigger half circle. For this to

Fig 6   *The horse looks in the direction in which he is going; having indicated right rein, the rider supports him by maintaining contact with the left rein.*

Fig 7   *The horse shows too much bend in the neck, with the head too much to the right and the rider slightly tilted to the right; the crossing of the back legs is lessened.*

happen, the horse's inside hind leg on the circle will cross over the outside hind leg, allowing him to make the bigger half circle.

First steps If you are making a half circle to the right, initiate your left incline by indicating with the left rein, while keeping contact with the right. When you are approximately three metres from the track, commence the half circle right by feeling with your right rein and supporting with your left. Immediately after signalling the change of direction,

put your right leg back behind the girth and try to keep your left leg as close to the horse's side as possible. If you then push with the right leg, the hind quarters will begin to make a bigger half circle as they move away from the pressure of the leg.

Naturally this exercise can only be done at the walk, and at walking pace the horse has plenty of time to consider your instructions. He may be a little confused as to your intentions, and he may not respond. If this happens, use your legs quicker rather than stronger to make him more responsive, and make sure your right leg is back far enough to influence the hind quarters only. If you do not go far enough back, the horse yields his whole body to the leg, creating a situation that defeats the purpose of the exercise.

Consolidation As an improvement begins, keep repeating the exercise but vary the distance you travel before starting the half circle. Do not allow the horse to anticipate the circle; make him understand that it comes when you say, not when he feels like it.

At the beginning you will probably find that this exercise is much easier on one rein than on the other. Your horse will probably try to hollow on his soft side, making it difficult to achieve any movement away from the leg. If this happens – and it almost certainly will – keep the contact on the opposite rein until you feel that the horse can move away from the pressure of either leg, in either direction. Once the half circle is completed, push the horse forward on to the straight line. If you let the movement fade away you will end up with a horse who only does three-quarters of what he is told. At all times the exercise must be purposeful, with a good, forward going walk; the horse must be in no doubt that he is working.

Leg Yielding

When you feel that you and your horse have mastered the reverse half volte, and the horse is responding to both of your legs equally, it is time to move on to leg yielding. Like the previous exercise, leg yielding is designed to teach the horse to yield to the pressure of a single leg and, as such, is a simplified version of the shoulder-in. Again, it is done at the walk (although it can be done later in trot) and it is easier if you have the luxury of a school in which to work, although this is not essential.

First steps A good way to start leg yielding is to make a ten- or fifteen-metre half circle at the end of the school, and then incline back to the long side you have just left. When you get to within two or three metres of the track, go parallel to it, while bringing the inside leg back to nudge the horse over until he is back on to the original line. Take care to keep the walk going all the time – especially at the moment when you ask the horse to yield.

When the horse begins to respond to the leg, try not to take it back quite so far, and continue shortening the backward movement until he is yielding to your leg in the normal riding position, with the stirrup leather vertical. This is because, unlike the reverse half volte, you want the horse to yield his whole body to your signal – that is, you want him to be going straight forward – and sideways at the same time. Eventually you should be able to dispense with the half circle and get the horse to yield to your leg whenever you ask him.

If you lack the advantage of an enclosed area you can practise this movement on a bridle-path or very quiet road by moving the horse to one side, and leg yielding him over to the other. This is very useful because it demands that he listens to you with his full concentration, something you want him to be doing when he is facing fences.

Vary the movement as much as possible, and make sure the horse is responding to your leg, and is not simply being

Fig 8 Leg yielding from left to right – the horse is as near to straight
as possible, allowing a marginal bend away from the direction of the movement.

drawn back to the track. To check this, try asking him to yield for two or three strides, and then to go forward for two or three strides. Repeat this several times, always varying the number of strides you use and then, just to reinforce the fact that you are in charge, leg yield him away from the track rather than towards it. Remember, however, that he must only leg yield for the number of strides that you actually ask of him. If you are not telling him to leg yield, he should be going straight forward. If the horse ever leg yields of his own accord, it is an evasion, and you must again start to make him respond only to your commands.

The great advantage of this exercise, once it has been mastered, is that it gives you so much more control. When you have the ability to limit your horse's movements to his hind quarters, you are in complete control of his impulsion. All a horse's power comes from behind, and when you can harness that power at will, you are really working as a partnership.

Consolidation Leg yielding and shoulder-in, with counter canter, are probably the only times when the horse is allowed to look away from the direction in which he is travelling. If you are leg yielding to the right, try to keep a light contact on both reins to minimise any tendency to bend; if there is any bend, make sure it is to the left. During the movement the right leg maintains a supporting role only. This means, that as you increase the pressure with your left leg, and the horse begins to yield, he should be as near straight as possible with the movement equally forwards and sideways.

If you are on virgin sand when you are doing this, you will notice that there are four distinct tracks. This is because in leg yielding to the right, the left foreleg will cross over in front of the right foreleg and the left hind leg in front of the right hind leg. The ideal pattern is four separate tracks, regular and evenly spaced.

By now you should have recognised that your legs control the hind quarters and the reins control the forehand; it follows that, by co-ordinating leg and hand, you can make both ends of the horse go in the same direction at the same time, and at the same speed. If the forehand goes quicker than the rear, the horse will make an incline towards the track and, conversely, if the hind quarters go more quickly, you will end up going away from the track. It is all a matter of balance, a balance which can be elusive.

For some time when you begin this exercise, you may have to do a bit of juggling to find out how much work you need to do at each end. The more you work, the more you will improve and from a showjumping point of view, this movement is only a preliminary to the more important exercise of shoulder-in.

Shoulder-in

Shoulder-in is an essential component of dressage, but for showjumpers, it is simply a very useful schooling exercise. If done correctly, shoulder-in requires the horse to move forward with his body at 30 degrees to the direction of the movement and – again working on wet sand – it should make three tracks. For right shoulder-in, the near hind leg makes one track, the near foreleg and off hind leg, going one in front of the other, make a single track, and the off foreleg makes a track of its own: three visible tracks in all.

From a straight line, the idea of this exercise is to encourage the horse to bring his shoulders in to the school, rather than to push his quarters out. There will be bend when you do this, and some is required, but you will find that you have to do more work on minimising it than encouraging it, especially on the horse's soft side.

For showjumpers shoulder-in has various uses. It can be used as a suppling exercise, as part of the warming-up procedure, in which case you would probably ask the horse for a little less than 30 degrees, or it can be used to get more engagement and response to your leg. In this last case, it would be beneficial to aim for even more than 30 degrees.

First steps Start the exercise in walk, remembering that you eventually have to be able to do it in trot, and give the horse a couple of strides of leg yielding to give him the idea. Using the long side of your school, or a hedge or wall, walk the horse two or three metres out from the usual track. Leg yield back to the track and, as you reach it, vibrate the right leg (for right shoulder-in) on the horse's side while, at the same time, using both hands to bring his forehand slightly in off the track.

At the start do not try for too much angle; it is more important to keep the horse settled and you should concentrate on maintaining the rhythm of the walk. Two or three strides is enough to ask at first, and when you have finished asking, allow the horse to go forward from the shoulder-in angle, rather than pulling him back on to the straight line. It is much better for keeping him going, to follow

Fig 9   On a quiet road: the right shoulder-in, in a long outline.

the curve of the shoulder-in bend away from the track and circle back to the straight line. Naturally, if you have to use a road or bridle-path, you will not be able to do this, but you should still let the horse go forward as much as possible after you have finished applying the aids.

Consolidation When, after a few weeks, you reach the stage when you can hold the movement easily for four or five strides, keep going purposefully forward from the shoulder-in and continue to settle for less than 30 degrees of angle. Only when you can hold the rhythm, as well as maintain the movement, should you attempt to increase the angle.

Again, do four or five strides of the more acute angle before going forward as before, and continue the exercise until you are comfortably achieving shoulder-in for as many strides as you like. Progress slowly, however. Always attach more importance to rhythm than to angle. You can increase the angle as you become more proficient, but if you lose the rhythm you will never be able to do the exercise correctly. In addition, never try to snatch or swing the horse into the full 30 degrees. If you do this, you run the risk of losing forward impulsion and the horse will almost certainly become unsettled.

Once you are happy with the mechanics of this exercise, you can begin to think of outline and shape. When you

Fig 10 Left shoulder-in showing the contact kept with the right rein.

reach this stage, be sure to establish a symmetrical shoulder-in on both reins. To achieve this you may have to use marginally different aids, according to the rein you are on. You might find that on one rein you have to bring the leg back a little, to be able to make the angle. On the horse's soft side he may go hollow and offer you more bend than you want, in which case you will have to limit the bend slightly.

Variations When you have achieved a symmetrical shoulder-in on both reins, you can begin ringing the changes in the use of the exercise. One variation is to go from shoulder-in to lengthened stride. This encourages the horse to maintain his

Fig 11 *Right shoulder-in with a more rounded outline.*

impulsion and makes him less likely to lose the rhythm of his trot. Another exercise is to follow shoulder-in with circles. Start the exercise, make a fifteen-metre circle to return to the track and repeat it until you can reduce the diameter of the circle. Aim to make about ten strides of good shoulder-in, followed by a ten-metre circle back to the track. This is good practice for feeling the horse between your inside leg and outside hand.

If your horse is inclined to be crooked or one-sided, you can use shoulder-in to help him straighten, by pushing him against his own preference. If, for instance, your horse is stiff to the left on a circle to the right, you will feel that you can push your right leg into your left hand. On the other rein, however, the horse would still like you to be hanging on to the left rein, so shoulder-in exercises in this direction, and pushing the left leg into the right hand, will help him to overcome his problems.

Another useful variation is to start shoulder-in in the same position you would use to ask for canter, and to change up to canter when you stop asking for shoulder-in. In other words, for left shoulder-in, keep the left leg in the normal position with the stirrup leather vertical and the right leg marginally behind, to prevent the hind quarters swinging out. From this position you can make shoulder-in and go forward into canter, leading with the left foreleg. If you try this exercise, always aim to do it with the minimum of effort. Achieving the canter should be as simple and immediate as switching on a light. Remember that the canter aid is not a signal to increase impulsion. The impulsion to change from trot to canter should always be there, and you should never think of the transition from trot to canter as a speeding up process. The change in speed from working trot to working canter is about two m.p.h. – hardly noticeable. Instead of regarding this movement as a change in speed, think of the transition as nothing more than a change in the sequence in which the feet come into contact with the ground.

There are many more variations that you can try, some of which you will dream up for yourself, and these and the basic exercise are all essential to the understanding you reach with your horse. As well as the obvious advantage of suppling up his muscles, this exercise, perhaps more than any other, requires you to appreciate fully the meaning of having the animal between leg and hand, and allows you to feel with your hand the energy that you create with the leg. Once you have mastered this movement you will use it to add finesse to your riding, and it will ensure that as far as possible, you and your horse work as one.

Fig 12   Left shoulder-in seen from the side, showing the horse between the rider's leg and hand.

Half Halt

Books on riding invariably give different explanations of the half halt; in fact the movement has acquired a mystical element, especially amongst relatively novice riders. It need not have, and should not have, any of this mystique. The half halt is nothing more than a momentary arresting of the stride to indicate to the horse that something is about to happen. It is a signal from rider to horse that more attention is required, or it tells the horse that something is wrong – the horse may be going too fast or too slowly, for instance – and the rider requires it put right. Half halting is also used, for example when striding a fence, to use up a half stride in the approach to a jump. If you are three and a half strides out when approaching a jump, it is better to use up the half stride in a half halt and jump off a full stride, than to be left with just a half stride when you reach the obstacle.

First steps Like most movements, half halting is learned at the walk. Start your horse walking purposefully in a straight line, with your legs close to the horse's side, but without actually pushing on. Close your fingers on the reins and then soften them immediately, so that there is no resistance in the animal's mouth and, at the same time, push on a little firmer with both legs. Keep the contact with both reins, to follow the movement as you feel the horse surge forward.

To begin with, it is likely to take three or four strides to achieve the desired response and for the horse to answer the check with the fingers. It must always be a check – never succumb to the temptation to make it a hard pull. Start with three or four little finger checks over

three or four strides, then over two strides and, eventually, in half a stride. No matter how long it takes, however, always proceed after the half halt actively, in whatever pace. Always try to maintain rhythm and outline throughout the movement and be vigilant for any evasions. If your horse lifts his head up and has a hollow back, or shows any other signs of resistance or discomfort, it is likely that you have set your hand, as opposed to making the signal and following the movement.

In trot, the movement is pretty much the same. Again, trot over two or three strides to start with – check, check, check followed by push, push, push – until you can go forward actively from a half stride. When the trot is mastered, attempt the same thing at canter using the same pattern of development.

Consolidation The practical use of this exercise, as well as the obvious one of controlling the striding to a fence, is to make the horse fully alert before any transition. A transition is a change of gait from one balanced, active pace to another – it is not a gradual slowing down or speeding up. At a given signal, the horse should respond immediately to the aids and change his gait. The horse can only do this if you open your fingers as soon as you have made the check. If you do not, you will confuse the horse; he will not really know whether you want the transition or not.

If, when making the transition from trot to walk, you almost stop, you have overdone the hand aid – check, give and push, check, give and push. It must become instinctive and, once it has, you will be able to bring a horse from canter to trot, with the horse trotting on alert, balanced, forward going and in rhythm. Ultimately you will be able to make your transitions 'missing a gear', from walk to canter or vice versa. When that happens, you know that the horse has been listening to you and has not merely interpreted your signals as 'speed up' or 'slow down'.

It is much better when schooling to run the risk of trotting or cantering a couple of extra strides, than to overdo the hand. If the transition does not happen, repeat the signal. Learn to trust your horse to respond and work towards lightness in your signals. It will take time but, in the end, you will have a horse who makes upward and downward transitions immediately, and with equal ease, upon request.

Outline

Horses must think that we humans are very perverse creatures when it comes to the outline we ask them to make. When a young horse goes along on his forehand with his head down, the natural position for a horse who spends most of his waking hours grazing, we ask him to come up off his forehand. However, as soon as he agrees to this request and brings his head and neck up, we reverse our request and tell him to bring his head down again.

The universal term 'on the bit' is misleading, because the shape we are trying to achieve is a perfectly vertical position of the head, which can be slightly behind the bit. A more accurate description would be to say that the horse is between leg and hand, and in a rounded outline.

Achieving Good Outline

A good outline should be rounded, and it should come from pushing the horse with the legs into a good contact. When this happens, the horse relaxes his lower jaw and flexes at his poll. In other words, the horse should not automatically drop his head on contact with the bit; he should only round his outline when he is ridden into it. If his head comes back when you are on a loose rein, you have taught him to over-bend. If you start to lower the horse's head too soon, you run the risk of lowering his neck as well. This has the effect of keeping him on his forehand, a position from which his impulsion cannot be engaged.

If the horse's neck goes straight out from his withers, you must try to get his hocks underneath him more, so that the greater engagement behind raises his forehand. Once he has raised his head and neck, you should try to lower just the head again, by encouraging him to relax his lower jaw and flex at the poll.

Preparation Remember that you are not interested in achieving the sort of shape that would be demanded of a top dressage horse. If your horse is working well between leg and hand, is supple and relaxed and doing some leg yielding and shoulder-in, the outline is likely to be the least of your worries. If you do ask for it, however, make sure that the horse is thoroughly worked in first. Every athlete needs warming up and stretching exercises before making a supreme effort, and the horse is an athlete. If you do ask too early, you will encourage him to look for evasions. He will raise his head, hollow his back, cross his jaw – anything to stop you from getting what he knows he is

Fig 13   This horse shows a poor outline – he is above the bit, hollow in his back and tracking short in trot.

Fig 14   A good outline – the horse is moving well between leg and hand.

unable to give. Even if your will is greater than his and you do achieve some sort of an outline, it will be a false one and will have been achieved at the expense of pace and length of stride. It will look wrong, it will confuse the horse and it will have defeated the whole purpose of the exercise.

Consolidation There is no doubt that when a horse is in the desired outline, he looks at his most noble but, once you have achieved the lowering of the head without the neck, do not hold the position for too long. If his muscles are not used to being in this position, they will soon get tired. As any movement is relief to a tired muscle, the horse will begin to move his head up and down and, if you allow this to continue, you will have taught him an evasion.

Don't get carried away with your success when you first feel him give his head to you. Ask only for very short periods of compliance and gradually increase the time, so that he has the opportunity to develop the muscles he needs to carry himself in this outline. Once the muscles are developed he will be happy to give you his head, and you will find that he is better prepared mentally, as well as more physically capable.

No matter how long you and your horse are capable of holding this outline, make sure you alternate it with sessions on a loose rein. He needs this time to stretch and relax the muscles – not only the muscles of his head and neck, but also the muscles behind the saddle which will have been built up by the more complete engagement of the hind quarters that this outline produces.

A good guide to how well you are schooling the horse for outline comes when you have him working in a circle between leg and hand. If you are on a left-hand circle and have the horse going from both legs into an even contact, try easing the right hand forward just an inch or two. You will find that he looks for the contact on the right-hand side and his head goes down and to the left as he looks for it. He will not raise his head and come above the bit.

This exercise will give you an idea whether you are pushing the horse into the outline or pulling him. It is also useful in other ways: if you ease your left hand forward on a left circle for a stride or two, and then take back the contact, you should find that the horse turns his head slightly to the right, looking towards the contact of the left rein. Ideally, if you were to soften both hands, the horse would lower his head forwards and downwards rather than escape from between leg and hand, but this is only possible with a very well-schooled horse. For most of us it is sufficient to have the horse yielding his head as he is pushed up with the legs. It is an aid to discipline, and an aid to jumping; after all, it is much easier to jump a horse with a steady head than one who tosses his head around continually.

Rider outline As a footnote to outline, remember that the rider has an outline too. A horse in the correct position can be spoiled by a sloppy looking rider. The rider's toe should be above the level of the heel, with the ankle relaxed. Concentrate on pulling the toes up into this position, rather than pushing the heels down. Pushing down tends to make the lower leg go forward and will create difficulties especially when giving the leg yielding aids. There should be two straight lines:

Fig 15   A longer, lower outline encourages the horse to stretch.

Fig 16   Although the horse is between leg and hand, he is technically wrong, being overbent.

the rider's shoulder – hip – heel, and the elbow, through the hand to the horse's mouth. Having achieved the correct position, the rider must hold his head up and look forward.

Advanced Work

Rein Back

Rein back is a measure of obedience and an excellent suppling exercise. As you would expect, it involves making the horse move backwards. Paradoxically, however, the horse should be thinking forwards as he moves, stepping backwards with his legs in diagonal pairs, at two-time pace.

Do not start this exercise until the horse is giving plenty of forward movement and you have him easily between leg and hand, in a good outline. Bring him to a halt and have him standing as near to square as possible, with a lowered head carriage and a relaxed lower jaw. When you are ready, close both legs on to his sides and close your fingers to resist forward movement. As you have created impulsion with your legs and resisted it with your fingers, the horse should step backwards.

Like everything in riding, do not ask for too much at once. Two or three steps backwards are enough to start with. When he has done a couple of strides back, open your fingers and, because you have kept your legs close to his sides, he will go forwards without a pause. Try not to rein back to a halt.

Corrections If your horse is capable of leg yielding and shoulder-in and is able to stand still with a lower head and a relaxed jaw, but still finds rein back difficult –

perhaps he resists in the mouth or puts his head up and hollows his back – other tactics are called for. Before you mount, and when you dismount, stand in front of him and, putting a hand on either side of the bit, gently push him back, saying quite firmly 'back' as you do so. Hopefully he will then start to associate the word 'back' with stepping backwards.

When the horse does this quite readily, try the exercise again mounted. Apply the aid and, as you do so, say 'back' firmly, until he realises what it is you want. After a while you will find that when you apply the aids he will anticipate the word and go back in response to this signal. When that happens, you can stop giving the verbal command.

If your horse reins back crookedly, for instance by swinging his quarters to the right, put him alongside a fence, hedge or wall and keep his shoulders as close to it as possible, while reining back. This helps the horse to help himself, the best possible way to train any animal. If his right shoulder is to the wall he cannot swing his quarters to the right. Some horses, however, will swing away from the wall on either rein, in which case you should put his left side close to the wall, close both legs and close the right fingers more firmly than the left. This should encourage him to move backwards in a straight line.

Flying Change

When you start work with a novice horse, he will probably favour leading with a particular leg in canter. Most horses are one sided, and prefer to canter with one leg leading than the other; the object of training is to encourage him to lead off with either leg, whichever you decide.

Similarly, when you start jumping, you will find the horse will probably favour one leg on which to land. You could be on right rein canter to a fence, with the off foreleg leading, and find that when you land the horse has changed to near foreleg leading canter. Obviously it is better that the horse takes off from and lands on the same leg, so if your horse does favour one leg, you must start considering being able to make a flying change.

Preparation Of all the movements we ask of a horse, this one should definitely not be begun too early. Do not attempt to teach a horse the flying change until he is quite at home with leg yielding, shoulder-in and the other demanding flat work exercises. To execute a flying change fluently, a horse must be athletic and supple, and he must be listening and willing to react immediately to every one of your aids.

Some horses will find this movement much easier than others – in fact, some will do it of their own accord. On changing direction when in canter, some will automatically change legs, but rather arbitrarily. More often a novice horse will become disunited when trying to change direction in canter. Clearly it is much better for you to be able to instruct the horse to change legs, and for him to do it whenever you ask him.

Method Before you attempt to teach any horse the flying change, start him off with a short jumping exercise. Set up a small rail, no more than two feet high, and put a pole on the ground on the landing side, set at an angle to the rail. Approach the jump in near foreleg leading canter, coming in on a slight incline from left to right. When you do jump, you will find, 99 times out of 100, that the angled pole on the ground has made the horse change to off foreleg leading canter. As you canter away from the fence, get a helper on the ground to change the angle of the pole and make a right-hand circle to approach the jump, again at a slight angle, this time from right to left. Jump the rail so that this time he canters off after the jump with his near foreleg leading again.

For younger and inexperienced show-jumpers, perhaps jumping a course for newcomers, it is better not to take the risk of losing balance and rhythm by trying a flying change. Better to bring the horse back to the trot before changing the canter leading leg. After a while, however, you will want to be able to change in canter pace. For this exercise you will need to be able to make transitions direct from walk to canter and from canter to walk.

Make a large figure of eight, change up from walk to canter, and, at the centre of the figure eight, execute a transition back to walk. Allow several strides of walking and change up again, bringing the horse back to walk at the central position. Gradually cut down the number of walking paces between changes until you can go canter, walk, canter with only one or two strides between the different leading legs.

Now you can start to give the horse signals to change his leading leg. This signal is made by changing the bend. When the off foreleg is leading, your bend is to the right so you feel the left rein and keep the right rein in support. You must, of course, allow and follow the change of bend and keep your left leg on the girth and your right leg back.

As the off foreleg leaves the ground at

Fig 17 Training for flying changes. The horse takes off in near foreleg leading canter.

Fig 18 Clearing the jump.

Fig 19   The positioning of a pole on the landing side of the jump influences the horse to change his canter lead.

Fig 20   Moving off in off foreleg leading canter.

the end of a sequence of right canter, nudge with your right leg to start the new sequence in near foreleg leading. Try not to change your weight too much as this will unbalance the horse and may make him become disunited. It is all a matter of timing: in canter, at the end of each sequence, there is a period of suspension, when no feet are on the ground at all; this is the moment to make the signal to restart on the other leg.

Flying changes are not always easy to master. They require a willing horse and a sensitive rider who is able to feel what the horse is doing underneath him. They also require patience and weeks of pains-taking work, as the horse learns to trust the rider and to understand the signals he is being given.

If there is a secret, it is never forgetting to allow for the other bend as you take up the left rein and bring the right leg back at the end of a right canter sequence. The whole movement is a little like swim-ming. For a time you cannot do it, and then, suddenly, you can and you wonder why it took so long.

The aids you are required to give are subtle and always need to be balanced on each side: taking up the left rein must be balanced with light contact on the right; nudging with the right leg must be bal-anced with firm girth contact on the left, and so on. Add these requirements to hav-ing to apply the aid at the precise moment of suspension, and you have an elusive combination. You must persevere: one day you will achieve it. Once the tech-nique is perfected, it is never forgotten.

Demi-pirouette

Unlike most of the other exercises dis-cussed here, the demi-pirouette, which is simply a turn on the haunches, cannot be performed at the trot. The sequence in which the horse moves his legs in trot makes it impossible for him to turn on his haunches in this pace. Consequently the movement is learned in walk, with the intention of stepping up into canter when the basics are mastered.

Uses There are various ways of turn-ing a horse: he can be turned on his forehand, with his back legs describing a circle around his front legs, or he can make a straightforward turn, where his back legs follow the track that his front legs have taken. He can also turn by moving his forehand around his hind quarters, showing a greater degree of control. The advantage of this method is that it is made with the hocks tucked well underneath the horse. This allows him to remain balanced, and to maintain the sequence of the walk or canter.

This is particularly useful in a jump-off against the clock when you are required to make a short turn, perhaps two or three strides from a fence. If you were to make such a turn on the forehand you would lose control of the hind quarters, which would probably result in the horse becoming disunited and in an impossible position regarding the fence. No matter how hard he tries, he will almost certainly have the fence down. If, on the other hand, you retain control of the hind quarters, and keep them active while maintaining the canter rhythm, you give the horse every chance of clearing the fence.

Preparation Two preparatory exer-cises are particularly helpful as leads into the demi-pirouette.

1. Make a half circle away from the track, fence, hedge or wall, whatever you are using as your straight guide – but do make sure it *is* straight. As you make the semi-circle, try to prevent the hind quarters from going outside the line that the front legs have taken; indeed, if possible, keep them just a little inside. To initiate the half circle to the left, open your left hand slightly and support it by laying the right rein on the horse's neck. At the same time put your right leg behind the girth to keep control of the hind quarters and the left leg on the girth to maintain the forward movement.

To open the hand, take it in the direction that you want to go. In other words, if you are making a half circle to the left, you will move the left hand 8-10cm to the left, to 'lead' the horse in that direction. This movement is distinct from pulling backwards on the left rein, which would inhibit the forward movement. Similarly, to support the horse with the right rein, you bring the rein marginally to the left so that it rests on the horse's neck; you must not make it a backwards pull.

To start with, the half circle should be approximately 3-5m. Once the horse is

Fig 21 Demi-pirouette – the forehand is coming round the hind quarters to the left, with the off foreleg crossing the near foreleg.

Fig 22 Demi-pirouette to the left – the rider's right leg is in position and the left rein is supported by laying the right rein on the horse's neck. The horse looks in the direction in which he is moving.

parallel to the track and facing in the opposite direction, continue the control with the right leg by leg yielding back to the original track. Carry out the exercise on both reins and try to reduce gradually the size of the half circle that the back legs are making.

Your main objectives are to keep the hind quarters of the horse working rhythmically and under control by the use of the right leg on the half circle left and the left leg on the half circle right. When the exercise is done at the walk you can try to cut down the size of the half circle until such a time as the hind quarters remain virtually on the same spot but continue to perform the sequence at the walking rhythm. This exercise, as a fairly advanced one, is only possible after you have mastered leg yielding and shoulder-in. Until you have done these exercises and you are able to move the horse away from the pressure of a single leg, you will not really have sufficient control over the hind quarters to prevent them swinging outwards. Only after you have succeeded in achieving the degree of control necessary for leg yielding and shoulder-in, will you be in a position to work towards demi-pirouette.

Make sure that you do not make the half circle too small to start with, and do bring the horse's forehand round using both hands. It is not enough to indicate left simply by feeling the left rein.

With the left hand slightly open, the horse is encouraged to bend in the direction in which he is going, but you want to be able to limit that bend without allowing him to hollow his neck. This is achieved by pressure from the right rein. It has the effect of almost pushing the forehand around to the left. If this is done in conjunction with the right leg going back behind the girth, the hind quarters will not be allowed to travel on a bigger half circle than that made by the front legs. It is this response to the right leg – the horse keeping his hind quarters in – which enables you gradually to cut down the size of the half circle. Ideally you will reach the stage where the horse bends in the direction in which he is going (but not too much), the hind quarters maintain the sequence of the walk and the balance and rhythm is unimpaired.

If you find that the horse does have a tendency to hollow his neck, you must try to limit that bend by keeping, in the case of half circles to the left, the pressure of the right rein as a support.

As with most other exercises, you will probably find these easier on one rein than the other to start with. However, the object of schooling the horse is to make his movements symmetrical on both reins. Avoid the tendency to rush things and do not succumb to the temptation of making the half circle too small to start with. If you do, the horse will either lose forward movement or pivot on his back feet. This is the last thing you want to happen because, if you are making a short turn in a jump-off against the clock and the horse pivots on his back legs, the feet remain on the ground instead of maintaining the rhythm of the canter. Without that rhythm, you create many more difficulties for yourself.

2. Make a 45 degree turn from the track as a preliminary to making a turn of 90 degrees. In giving the signals for the turns, you bring the forehand round while, at the same time, keeping control over the hind quarters so that they do not .

Fig 23 Demi-pirouette to the left – the horse maintains his walk rhythm.

leave the track or follow the track that the front legs have made.

Again, if turning to the left, open the left hand slightly, support with the right rein, bring the right leg behind the girth and bring the horse around at 45 degrees from the track, with the back feet continuing in the walking rhythm on the track. Work to keep the forward movement in the walk and, when it begins to feel quite easy, make a 90-degree turn. Use the same aids but keep them going throughout the 90 degrees and then go

forward, across the school, while maintaining a good walking rhythm.

Be patient with these exercises and bear in mind that they represent quite a lot of information for the horse to take in. Plan the exercises over several sessions rather than all in one go, and keep your objectives firmly uppermost in your mind.

Into Canter If you use both these exercises you should eventually be able to turn a little further round – perhaps a three-quarter turn, 135 degrees instead of 90 – before you go forward in the walk. At this stage you can start thinking about stepping the exercise up into canter.

In canter, as in walk, do not make your circles too small to begin with as this will encourage the horse to start swinging his hind quarters outwards against the pressure of your leg. Start with a 20-metre canter circle, perhaps reducing to a 15-metre circle, without allowing the hind quarters to swing out. When you are able to start with a 15-metre circle and easily cut it down to 10 metres, you can concentrate on reducing it still further – but take your time. Let the circles get smaller a little at a time, until you feel you can bring the forehand round the hind quarters, still maintaining rhythm, in something like a 5-metre canter circle. When you can do this, and keep your rhythm, you are well on the way to achieving the control that will allow you to perform quite a short turn into a fence during a jump-off. Indeed, you will probably find that two or three straight strides are all you need to be able to jump a fence quite comfortably.

2 Basic Jumping

It is not necessary for a horse to jump large fences for him to use his jumping muscles. He will exercise all the relevant muscles over quite small jumps, and the easier his work is, the more he will enjoy it. Obviously his training must be carefully planned – there is always something that needs working on – but big jumps are the end product of training, not the beginning.

Trotting Poles

Trotting poles are occasionally a more difficult exercise for a horse who has jumped, than for one who has never seen them before. This is because after jumping the horse thinks all poles, on the ground or in the air, must be taken at canter. No matter what stage of training your horse is at, it never does any harm to go back to basics occasionally; trotting poles, simple exercises though they are, can be very effective in sorting out your horse's trotting stride and relaxing him mentally.

Early Work

Even if your horse is quite experienced, never present him with four or five poles on the ground immediately. Start off with one pole and simply ask him to walk over it. As he does so, he will lower his head and neck and your job, as the rider, is to make sure that he maintains his walk rhythm throughout the movement. If the horse does slow the walk, throw his head up in the air or break into a trot or canter, making him walk the pole will be a valuable exercise. If he slows, nudge a little with your legs to preserve the forward movement, and perhaps trot away from the pole a couple of times until he can walk the pole easily and maintain his rhythm. If he tends to hurry, do not take him too far from the pole and keep your fingers 'breathing' a rhythm with the stride. Above all, keep him interested in your presence on his back, even if it means you have to move the bit gently around in his mouth.

Once you can walk one pole without problems, put down a second one, 2.75m from the first, and take them in trot. If he hurries, ask for something a little slower than working trot. One stride takes you over the first pole and then there is a natural trotting stride before he has to take the second pole. This, in itself, will help sort out any hurrying problems.

Do not worry if your horse lowers his head; it means that he is looking where he is going and that he is relaxing, both in the neck and in the muscles behind the saddle. Do not let any lowering of the head sabotage the rhythm, however, or slow the forward movement. Keep him going forward all the time.

Occasionally you will need to make small adjustments. If your horse is a little close to a pole, he might have to shorten slightly, and if he is too far away he will have to stretch; neither movement is wrong. Indeed, if anything, both are good in that they teach you the feeling of following the movement changes that come with any variation in stride.

When you have negotiated two poles a few times, add another, again 2.75m away. An adjustment of a few centimetres either way may help, but most horses will find it easy to trot three poles 2.75m apart. If you do have to modify, make your changes only centimetres at a time until you have found the striding that is comfortable for the horse.

Once the distance is established, put new poles between the three poles already on the ground and add another one, 1.3m away from the last pole. This will give you a row of six poles, all 1.3m apart; six pole-trotting strides, in fact. At this stage, the horse should be able to trot the six poles at a comfortable working trot pace while being calm, attentive, active and aware of where his feet are going.

Variations

As the exercises progress, the interest of the horse is bound to wander. He knows that once he is in the poles he simply has to trot to come out unscathed, so now is the time to wake him up again – to make him more active without increasing his speed. There are several ways of doing this. Some trainers like to vary the

Fig 24   The horse trots over three poles, each 2.75m apart, making one trotting stride between each pole.

Fig 25   Having filled in the gaps, the horse is now trotting over six poles approximately 1·3 metres apart.

distance between the poles, but I prefer to raise them slightly. You can do this by raising one end of the fourth pole, for example, by about 30-45cm, putting it on a stand of some sort. The effect of this is that the horse has to look again at what he is doing and you must again work on keeping the rhythm throughout, despite your horse's curiosity and possible wariness over the new element. Next, take the third pole and raise that at the opposite end to the fourth pole so that they make a shallow 'V' in the middle of the combination. Continue this process until all the poles are raised at alternate ends so that, as the horse approaches, the poles look like a 'V' channel.

Most horses will have got the idea by this stage, but if you lose the rhythm or have difficulty starting the sequence, put a rail flat on the ground 1.3m in front of the first inclined pole. This will give him an easy stride before he has to produce a more elevated trot for the raised poles.

This is an excellent exercise in many ways but do have someone on the ground with you at all times – not only for safety, which is important, but to move the poles. If you have to dismount continually to change the pattern, you will lose the continuity of the exercise; if, however, you do about half an hour of this exercise with ground help, your horse will be stronger, more supple, more mentally alert and you will have made the point that increased activity need not necessarily mean more speed.

Advanced Sequences

The next time you go out, you can take the trotting pole exercises a little further.

Fig 26   Negotiating raised trotting poles.

Fig 27   Having started with only one pole raised, four of the six poles are now alternately higher at one side, presenting a 'V' effect in the middle.

Fig 28   All six trotting poles in the sequence are now raised.

Fig 29   Note the flexion of the horse's knee and hock joints.

Gradually make your raised trotting poles 1.15m apart instead of 1.3m (having, of course, worked up from poles on the ground, and raising the poles one at a time); 4.75m from the last pole, make a simple crossed-pole jump, no more than 45cm high in the centre. This will be as much a test for you as for the horse, in that as you trot the poles in rising trot, you must concentrate on sitting between the last trotting pole and the crossed pole jump. If you do not and you are concentrating on the jump itself after the last trotting pole, you will not be able to put in the little gathering canter stride. Your thoughts will have communicated themselves to the horse and unbalanced him. Remember that this exercise is designed to ask the horse to be patient so be patient yourself and wait for the jump to come to you.

If you progress at the average rate, you will be able to raise the crossed poles to about 75cm in the centre quite quickly; follow this with a back rail, just higher than the crossed poles, with a spread about the same as the height at the centre of the cross. The size, height and spread will depend on the experience of the horse and rider but, when you have consolidated and are happy with whatever you have set up, add a single rail jump, the same height as the back rail of the crossed pole/rail spread, 6m on from the first jump. This will give you your trotting poles, a gathering canter stride, a hop over the first jump, a non-jumping canter stride and a pop over the last. If all goes well you can immediately make the last jump a parallel, to get the horse

Fig 30   The raised trotting poles are followed by one non-jumping canter stride to a small fence.

stretching more into his work.

Finally, and only when you are sure the horse is ready, start inching the front rail of the parallel closer to the back rail of the first fence, making the distance between the jumps shorter. At the same time, make the spread of the parallel slightly wider. This will force the horse to be quicker in picking up his front legs and will make him push a little more off his hocks to clear the spread, again giving you more action without more speed.

All of these exercises put the horse into situations where he has to use his own natural abilities, as well as giving him more confidence, in himself and in his rider; they are *not* designed to test his confidence. Never ask him for too much, and make your changes slowly so that each movement is only slightly different from the previous one. If you do this, exercises over poles will help to give you a confident horse, capable of tackling any new challenge that you put before him. These are the very qualities that every showjumper requires.

Grid Work

Grids are particularly useful training aids. With grids, the trainer can work on the rider's position; he can work the rider without reins or without stirrups, and he can concentrate on developing the correct seat. Grids also remove the necessity for the rider to see a stride, and therefore take away any anxiety that leads to tenseness. By consistently taking off in the same place, the rider gets the feel of what he will be looking for when he rides free to a single fence. The exercise will eventually help the rider to be able to see a stride.

For the trainer, the bounce grid of four or five rails is almost like seeing the rider jump one jump in slow motion. It is essential for spotting faults and working out how to put them right. Grids also encourage the horse to maintain the rhythm of his canter in approach and, on a small scale, help him to overcome any problems with double and treble combinations when the time comes for jumping a proper course.

In one-stride grids, keep the distance between the elements shorter than normal: 6.5m perhaps, rather than the normal 7.5m. The shorter distance discourages speed and encourages the horse to jump off his hocks. At the beginning, however, do all you can to make things easy for the horse; if he is naturally long striding, make the distances slightly longer, and vice versa for the short strider. Once they have settled in, and know what is required, gradually adjust the distance, either longer or shorter, and just a few centimetres at a time, until they are using themselves properly over the shorter distance.

As a variation, allow the horse to jump in his own balance on a loose rein, to give him confidence in his own ability, so that he does not expect the rider to work for him all the time. Alternatively, maintain contact while following the movement as the horse stretches his head and neck by staying in balance and keeping the horse between leg and hand.

All grid work depends upon the surface on which you are jumping. Grid exercises are repetitive and should not be done when the ground is rock hard, even though the low grids do not give the same jar as the bigger fences.

Stride Grids

If you ride out with the intention of doing grid work, or any other form of jumping for that matter, it should not be necessary to ride in for half an hour before you attempt anything. At this stage in your development, both you and the horse should have got used to the routine of jumping as part of your daily work, so you can ride him in for five minutes and then continue his warming up work over small and easy jumps.

Early work Start off with a rail no more than about 45cm high, with a trotting pole 2.75m in front. The trotting pole is really optional, but if you want to make sure the horse is thinking about what he is doing, it can be a good idea. Approach the jump in a good working trot, concentrating on achieving the ideal of 'calm activity', and follow the movement as the horse makes what will be not much more than a fairly large canter stride over the little jump. Do this half a dozen times but, on the landing side, vary the canter away. On landing the horse will be in canter, and you should keep him cantering until you tell him to trot. Try never to let him know when this moment will be. Sometimes bring him back quite soon, other times ask him to canter a circle before making another trot approach. In other words, keep him thinking and do not let him anticipate your aids. If, however, the horse has a tendency to hurry his canter away, it is best to bring him back to a trot quickly but gently on the landing side.

As soon as everything is in order and you are performing the jump straight and quietly, add another rail, also 45cm high, 6.5m from the first, to give a jump–stride–jump combination. Settle into this – three times on each rein should be sufficient – and then add a third rail, also 6.5m away. Now you will have jump–stride–jump–stride–jump.

Variations Apply the same pattern as before, three approaches to this combination on each rein if all is going well, and maintain a comfortable rhythm throughout. To keep the horse interested and to make progress, you can then proceed to an ascending grid. Raise the middle rail of the grid a couple of holes and the final rail about four holes. This will have the effect of slightly shortening the distances between the obstacles and will make the horse work just that little bit harder. It will also encourage him to come off his forehand, as he has to come through from behind to achieve that little bit of extra height.

When he is doing this to your satisfaction, you can add the complication of ground lines. Put poles on the ground about 30cm in front of each rail. They will make him look, and if he lowers his head to do so then so much the better, but do not let him slow or quicken the pace. The ground poles should not bother a reasonably experienced horse, but a novice might want to take a close look and you should let him get thoroughly accustomed to ground lines before raising all the jumps. This time each jump should be raised by the same amount, about 5cm. Each jump will be slightly higher, but the ascending effect remains.

When this is no problem, change the appearance of the jumps again. This time you could raise one end of each ground line pole into cups; the best way is as with the trotting poles, raising the right end of the first one, the left end of the second

Fig 31   Jumping a sequence of three rails, each 6.5m apart.

Fig 32   The horse makes one non-jumping stride between each element.

46

Fig 33   *Jumping out of the sequence; all rails are the same height.*

one, and so on. The height of the rise should be a few holes above the rail so that there is a reasonable angle. This will change the appearance of the grid considerably, but if you are jumping where you should – in the middle of each jump – the height will not be changed at all.

The next step is to make the last jump of the grid into a spread. Add a rail, a hole or two above the front rail to continue the ascending effect, and make the spread about the same as the height of the new rail – about 1.1m. This is not an enormous jump, but the horse will have to be jumping it properly because of the grid constraints you have placed upon him. It is an easy and painless way, indeed the best way, of introducing any horse to a fence of reasonable size.

Less experienced horses will probably be ready for a break by this stage and, providing you end on a high note, you can pat him and take him home. More experienced horses, however, can be given a few more changes to keep them interested.

Advanced work   Try keeping the same distances but ask the horse to jump high-sided cross poles, instead of rails. The advantage of this is that the cross helps to keep the horse in the middle of the fence, and it encourages him to tuck up more neatly with his front legs while keeping his feet close together; it is an excellent exercise for teaching a horse to fold correctly.

With all these exercises, distances and heights are approximate and very much dependent on the level and overall ability of rider and horse. However, if you have been riding the horse for any time at all, the horse's mental attitude to work, including discipline, should be reflecting

47

Fig 34   Beginning an ascending stride grid – the first element is
unaltered.

Fig 35   The second element is two holes higher than the first.

Fig 36   The distance between the elements is unaltered.

48

Fig 37   A ground line has been introduced on the raised fences.

Fig 38   The third element is four holes higher than the first.

your own. The exercises themselves involve a certain discipline in that they are repetitive; in grids you repeatedly do things as near perfectly as possible. You do not have to worry about the striding, and your horse does not have to worry about the height of the jumps, so you can both continue doing grid after grid until correct and tension-free jumping is almost second nature.

Bounce Grids

Bounce grids are excellent for conditioning a horse's jumping muscles, and should be approached, at the outset, in very much the same way as stride grids. Set up a single rail, between 30 and 45cm high (take-off pole optional) and jump it two or three times on each rein. Follow the usual pattern of ringing the changes on the landing side – slow him down quite briskly if he is charging through, or push him on if he is hesitating, and make him concentrate on his work.

Fig 39   An ascending stride grid of three elements, with high-sided cross poles.

Fig 40   Clearing the second element.

Fig 41   There is one non-jumping canter stride between each element.

Fig 42   Clearing the last element in the sequence.

Fig 43 A back rail is introduced to the final element of the ascending
stride grid with high-sided cross poles.

Fig 44 The back rail encourages the horse to bascule.

Early work Once you have established the first rail, add another approximately 3.25m from the first, and at the same height. Having done stride grids the horse will not be surprised at having to jump two rails quite closely, so you can approach exactly as before. The difference is that this time you have quite a large canter stride for the first rail, followed immediately by another canter stride to jump out. The landing of the first is the take-off for the second.

If you and the horse can manage this with confidence, with the horse calm and active and paying attention, add another rail, at the same height, 3.25m from the second – this distance can be varied depending on the distance most suitable for your horse. If the distance is right, the horse will be able to maintain a good rhythm and his canter bounces will appear quite effortless. The distance between the poles is, in fact, a little shorter than would be considered normal for a horse in working canter. Most horses make a stride of between 3.45 and 3.75m in this gait; however, we are asking the horse to make a little more height over the rails than he would normally make in working canter, and this has the effect of shortening his stride. To assess your own ideal distance, concentrate on making sure that your horse does not have to stretch or shorten his stride dramatically; it should look natural for him.

Developing a sequence When you have done two bounces add a fourth rail and then a fifth in fairly rapid succession. Four rails will do, but five is a better number for making more progress later on. For example, once you are both comfortable and jumping fluently down a line of five, you can take the fourth rail

and make a parallel with it on the inside of the fifth pole. This will give you a distance of between 6.25 and 6.5m, or a non-jumping canter stride between the third bounce pole and the spread. Make the rails on the spread a couple of holes higher than the bounce rails and, to start with, make it ascending, with the back rail higher than the front.

Now canter the line, evenly and rhythmically, and establish the new grid before changing the look of it again with a pole on the ground in front of the spread. This is purely to change the appearance and it should have no effect on the horse's attitude at all.

The next step is to take out the third bounce rail. This will leave you with a bounce, two non-jumping canter strides and the final spread. Try, during the non-jumping strides, to keep the canter even so that all the strides of the grid are the same length. The horse will have been helped in this by the regularity of the exercises and most will willingly canter through on an even rhythm and stride. Some, however, will want to put in a long one and a short one, in which case you may have to go back to a line of bounces before reintroducing non-jumping strides.

If all goes well, however, raise the parallel, which effectively shortens the distance and encourages the horse to jump more off his hocks. Once you can make a good, parallel jump after two even non-jumping strides, it is time to conclude; if you start taking more rails out, you are involving related distance (*see* Chapter 3). Two non-jumping strides are sufficient, especially if the purpose of the exercise is to establish balance.

Throughout these exercises we have

Fig 45   The horse jumps the second element of a bounce grid of five rails.

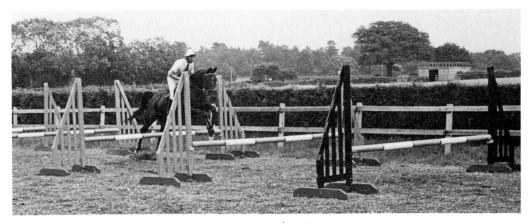

Fig 46   The third element – all elements are approximately 3.25m apart and all are the same height.

Fig 47   The fourth element.

been concentrating on producing a metronome-like rhythm from a horse in a calm frame of mind. This is ideal, but do not let him, or yourself for that matter, go to sleep. If you think he needs livening up, try dismantling the grid and asking him to jump just one brightly coloured small showjump filler. After being conditioned to expect a line of jumps, with his take-off predetermined, he will be very wary of the filler; be purposeful so that he knows that although it looks different, it will not harm him.

Rider's Grid Work

Rider's position You have used grid work to work on the canter rhythm and to perfect the horse's technique, but what about you, the rider? You too can use the grid to work on your own position. A five-rail bounce grid is excellent for exercises with no reins and no stirrups; the rider simply concentrates on his own position. After doing this a few times, bring the stirrups and reins back and soften the hand, loosening the rein two or

Fig 48   The fourth element is moved to the fifth element, making a small spread fence. This leaves three bounce rails and one non-jumping canter stride, followed by a jump over the small spread.

Fig 49   The first two bounce rails remain as before.

Fig 50   The third bounce rail has been removed to make a filler for the small spread.

Fig 51   There are now two non-jumping canter strides before the small spread.

Fig 52   The second non-jumping stride.

Fig 53   The small spread is now slightly larger and more challenging than before.

three strides out from the grid. This will allow the horse to jump down the line in his own balance, at his own rhythm and pace, and with no contact on the mouth.

Doing a grid on a loose rein is not the end product of any exercise. The culmination you are aiming for is to be able to ride the whole grid – approach, fences and landing – with the horse between leg and hand. So, after a loose rein line, take up a light but constant contact with both reins and allow your hands to follow whatever distance the horse wants to stretch his neck (making sure, of course, that your hands follow towards his mouth). Fortunately the horse will not stretch his head too much down a bounce or stride grid, so you will be able to practise feeling the stretch and allowing a moderate amount.

Changing the leading leg When you work over straight-line grids, you will probably find that the horse will land favouring one particular leading leg. Do not worry about this too much, as there is no sense of direction on the straight line; you are not thinking of making a tight turn to approach another fence, so it is best to keep the canter in the horse's leading leg. In fact, you will find that most horses will land in near foreleg leading canter if they come off the right rein and off fore-leg leading canter if they come off the left rein.

At this stage, providing that there is no physical reason why the horse is favouring one leg more than the other, there is no need to worry. If you, the rider, have a sense of direction and purpose on the landing side of a fence, and if the horse is balanced, the horse will probably follow your sense of direction and land with the correct leg leading. You can influence this by looking in the direction in which you intend to go. If, despite this, you consistently land on the near foreleg, for example, do not worry. With continued use of the exercises that you are doing on the flat, and with the better balanced horse that you are producing with your grids, the time will come when the horse will pick up your sense of direction and land on the correct leg, without you having to do any more.

Planning In the early days it is essential to concentrate fully on the aspect of work you have chosen for the day – horse's style over a fence, rider's position over a fence or some other point. Neither you nor the horse can think of everything at any one time, so choose one target area and attack it; you can always attack another target tomorrow. However, whatever you choose to work on, be sure to vary the place where you ask the horse to return to trot after the grid. Occasionally bring him back quite quickly, but work towards letting him canter on quietly in a circle (on the leg on which he has landed) so that he gets used to being in a good rhythm for the time when another fence is presented to him, perhaps half-way round the circle. Establish a pattern of landing and going quietly on at a speed and at a rhythm that could easily be the approach to another fence.

There will be times during grid work when the horse will put his head down, shrug his back, and feel pleased with himself. Do not worry – and certainly do not pull his head up – unless he is putting his head down and deliberately bucking in an attempt to get you off. If he is simply expressing his enjoyment and canters along with his back shrugged, pulling him up too quickly will inhibit his hind quarters over the fence. Let him enjoy his moment of relaxation and then quietly restart him when he has settled.

Finally, use common sense when you ask your horse to do grid exercises. If the ground is hard, do not continue working him in an attempt to get something right. The great thing about grids is that you can work on a pattern without having to jump large obstacles, but all obstacles take their toll, and particularly on hard ground. Attempt grid work for twenty minutes on three consecutive days, rather than a full hour at the start. With shorter periods the horse will be fresher, and you can virtually restart at the point where you finished the day before. An hour will tire him and, worse, run the risk of boring him, when he will begin to look for evasions at every opportunity.

Training Uses

Grids are for the benefit of both horse and rider. They establish correct habits through repetition and they are essential for the training of a good showjumper. Choosing between bounce and stride grids, bounce grids are probably preferable; they bring so many benefits. Mistakes, when they occur, glare at you from a bounce grid line: because the rider has no time to go forward and up at every jump, he takes the jumping position at the first rail and keeps it until the grid is

Fig 54   The author rides through a bounce grid without reins or stirrups.

*Fig 55   The rider must adjust his position at the jump to maintain
balance and control with the legs.*

Fig 56 Note the folding of the arms – right hand on left elbow, left hand on right bicep, facilitating an immediate right hand grip on the reins or neckstrap if necessary.

finished. For the trainer it is like seeing the rider in slow motion. Faults can be picked up and corrected as the rider makes his way down the line.

For the horse, the grid establishes the pattern of a smooth canter rhythm that remains the same, even when the final spread is increasing a little in size. It teaches novice horses, and novice riders, that more height does not require more speed – if that was the case, a 2.25m high *puissance* would require an approach the length of an airport runway. Grids show riders that by maintaining canter rhythm at the same time as the fence is raised, the jump simply becomes an extension of the canter stride – no matter whether it is rounded over an upright or more stretched over a spread.

Seeing a Stride

'Seeing a stride' involves the rider's eye and what is happening around him in any given circumstance. If, on approaching a fence, your eye tells you that you are three and a half strides away, it is obviously better to make a half halt and go half, one, two, three, rather than one, two, three, and leave the horse in difficulties half a stride wrong at the fence.

Some people are born with the ability to estimate striding distances but, equally, there are people who can never see a good stride. Nevertheless, I am convinced that striding a horse to a fence can be worked on; I am also convinced that many of the people who claim not to be able to see the stride can, in fact, do so, but refuse to allow themselves to believe what they see, with the result that they get

61

the horse wrong at the fence.

There is one cardinal rule to seeing the stride: if you cannot help by adjusting the horse on the way to the fence, never hinder him by making uncertain and frequent adjustments as you approach. Simply concentrate on speed and steering, and let the horse sort the jump out for you.

Problems

It is easy to notice from the ground when a rider sees a stride. His eyes light up and there is invariably a distinct movement of legs and/or hands. If the horse still meets the fence wrongly, or simply jumps it badly, then the rider is contrite and apologetic.

Sometimes it is, of course, the rider's fault. He saw the correct stride but failed to give the signal clearly or purposefully. The horse could not respond quickly enough to the weak signals and was wrong at the fence because of incorrect execution of the aids – not because the rider's eyes misjudged the stride.

One of the problems about teaching riding, and learning for that matter, is communicating exactly what is required. Over the years the sport has developed its own jargon, and riders and trainers alike use it. For example, the commonly used phrase 'set the horse up' is misleading; if a horse is between leg and hand, and making a nice, balanced, working canter stride he is already set up. If you approach a fence in 'set up' working canter, and the horse, of his own accord, lengthens, shortens or gains a stride, or loses impulsion, you are likely to meet the fence wrongly despite being 'set up'.

Too many people begin to worry if they cannot see a stride five or six strides away from the fence, and they convey their uncertainty to the horse. Through this anxiety, the horse receives a series of conflicting signals – yes, no, wait, maybe – and then the rider wonders why the horse goes wrong at the fence. You have only to see a top horse and rider combination turn off one or two straight canter strides to a big parallel fence, to realise how futile it is to worry six or seven strides out. If you are going to be wrong at a fence, it will not be too bad if the horse is in balance and a good rhythm, with the proper amount of impulsion. The horse will at least be in the position of being able to help you out, whereas he cannot help if you have perplexed him with contradictory signals in the approach. The course designer will occasionally set out his obstacles with the intention of catching you out. Their job is, after all, to get a result without going too high or wide, so there will be several fences that cannot be jumped properly unless an adjustment is made; there will also be some fences that are met spot on, without any adjustment at all. It is up to you to tell the difference, and being able to see the correct stride will help you enormously.

Developing Technique

To assist the development of your technique, start with a small vertical fence, of a size which is relative to your experience and that of your horse. Approach the fence at working canter, keeping your eyes on the highest part of the fence, and make one decision on striding which must be seen through to the end of the jump. If the fence is small, there is no need to go too far away from it to start with – a shorter approach will give you less time in which to change your mind – but as you progress, start to approach from further out without changing the canter rhythm.

Most horses will put up with quite a lot, but what they cannot tolerate is indecision and, for this reason, it is not advisable to make two half strides on the way to a fence. Two half strides might just as well have been one proper one, and a full stride is encouraging to a horse; two half strides simply tell him that you are indecisive and they interfere with his balance and rhythm.

Ideally the horse should take off as close to the fence as possible, providing that he has enough room to fold his legs and clear the jump. However, there is some leeway. With your eye, you can ride into a 'take-off zone' which is about a half stride in depth. You may end up a little close to the fence or, on the other hand, a little too far off, but neither is wrong provided that the horse has been ridden with purpose into the zone.

For this reason, you should ride at the fence and follow the movement as the horse jumps. Do not forget that jumping is the horse's job, not yours. Ride with purpose, stay with the movement and in balance, and interfere with the horse as little as possible.

Rider's hand position The position of the rider's hands in a perfect jump is similar to that of a transition: they should be in contact with the horse's mouth but at the same time light and soft enough to follow the movement as the horse stretches his head and neck forward and down, allowing in turn the hind quarters to 'float' over the fence. When horses bascule over a fence, each is individual in how much the neck will lengthen and so it is impossible to say exactly how many centimetres forwards you should move your hands; you must allow as much rein as your horse needs.

Here are some variations on the theme of allowing or following with your hands:

1. The hands follow the movement of the horse's head and mouth, which ties in with the flat work position of a straight line from the elbow through the hand to the horse's mouth.
2. The hands are pushed up the horse's neck towards his ears (known as the 'crest release' in the USA) which gives the jumping horse sufficient rein to drop his head and round over the fence.
3. A style used by some riders (perhaps those whose horses are a shade slower over the ground and make a more explosive effort on take-off) is to keep one hand near the horse's withers and put the other hand round the front of the horse's neck to provide something on which to anchor themselves. There are those who favour an increase in rein pressure as the horse is taking off to pull him off the ground, but this is inclined to inhibit the horse's hind quarters so it can work against you.
4. Some riders drop their hands towards the horse's front feet and can allow enough rein using this technique, although it is probably difficult to maintain balance.

Whatever system you find works best for you, the most help you can be to your horse when he is jumping an obstacle is to minimise any interference with the process. Do what you have to – but no more.

Variation Once a balanced technique has been achieved at small fences, attempt some larger ones, perhaps adding a back rail to make a spread. If this option is taken, it is best to make the back rail a hole higher than the front one, so that the fence appears to be ascending. This is a test for the rider. The tendency will be to fix the gaze at the highest element – the back bar. This is wrong: when the fence is approached, the eyes should be on the highest part of the front element, which has to be cleared first and which therefore conditions the take-off.

Faults and corrections If, despite giving the horse all the positive help that you can, he still stands off too far or puts in an extra stride, the answer is to work on the canter itself. If your tendency is to get too close, concentrate on making your canter slightly longer; if you stand off, then try to round him up a little. Again, this is a matter of patience, but you will find that the more regular your approach to fences is, the more consistently you will see the stride.

As a general rule, a longer canter tends to put the horse too far off the fence, or far enough off for him to consider putting in a short stride; a more rounded canter is usually more suitable. However, the roundness must not be overdone. Many riders, thinking they are three and a half strides out, put in a half stride, overdo the check and still finish long, with the horse having to stand off. The answer is always to use just as much adjustment as is needed – too much and you give yourself some other problem.

The great thing about horses is that if they are going to make a mistake or do something wrong at a fence, they are as likely to do it at a small fence as they are at a larger one. The difference, of course, is that a mistake is less disastrous at a small

fence, so if jumping mistakes are evident, 80cm is a better height than 1.3m for sorting them out.

I cannot emphasise too much that to see a stride you must look at the fence. It is no good gazing through the horse's ears at the distant horizon – no one has ever seen a stride by looking at the top of the oak tree in the next field. It is true that some people find striding easier if they look at the place where they want the horse's feet to land in the take-off zone. The method that suits you will only be found by experimentation, but work on looking at the fence first, as this works for the majority of riders and it will, most likely, work for you.

Balance

I am often amused by riders who tell me their horses have a tendency to rush their fences. When I see them ride, I invariably find that the riders themselves are some way in front of the movement. The horses are not rushing, they are simply trying to keep up with their riders. The ideal is to be in balance, but if you are going to be wrong, be behind the movement rather than in front of it – the horse will thank you for it. The worst way to be left behind is to get in front of the movement. Almost all riders concentrate on not being left behind, and become so anxious about this that they get themselves in front of the movement.

Problems

When the horse is between leg and hand and the contact suddenly disappears, the horse will put his head down to look for the bit. By being in front of the movement, your weight comes forward a fraction too early at the jump. This overburdens the horse's forehand and, instead of taking off, he is forced to put in a final short stride; this puts him even more on to his forehand and throws you even more out of balance. The inevitable result is a cat jump which, because of the violent change of speed, will throw you backwards and cause you to give the horse an enormous yank on the mouth. Not surprisingly, the next time this situation arises the horse may decide that it is safer to stay on the ground and not to risk jumping, and you have, in effect, taught him to refuse.

Compared to this situation, being slightly behind the movement is no problem. You have ridden the horse forward until he is in the air and, although he has taken off a split second before you, no great harm has been done. Provided you keep your hands down and slip (let go of) the reins, the horse will not even notice the mistake, unless, of course, you draw it to his attention.

Correcting take-off problems   Always remember that the leeway in the take-off is a full half stride. No horse can ever be more than half a stride wrong at a jump. If he is three-quarters of a stride out in one direction, he is only a quarter of a stride out in the other, so the maximum you can be wrong is 1.5-1.75m (half a stride) and this is neither here nor there at a small jump.

The lesson here is that you should not be too critical of yourself if there are variations in the take-off zone. You can stand off a little, or be a fraction too close, and still be on the correct stride. Too much self-criticism will be communicated to the horse; he should not be taught that

take-off must always be on the same blade of grass. If you do this you make a rod for your own back. If, however, you are positive and accept that there will be variations at take-off, you will find that the horse sorts out those little differences without you really being aware of it.

On the other hand, there is nothing worse than setting off on a lengthening stride and either changing your mind, or letting the horse put in a short last stride. This puts him on his forehand, loses forward movement and makes it very difficult for him to jump the fence. If you keep the lengthened stride, the horse is in no doubt what you intend, and you will find that he is not as far off when you reach the fence as you thought. If you retain the long stride, he will certainly not be able to creep into the bottom of the fence and no doubts about your intentions occur to him.

If your horse does put in a short stride, but still clears the fence, do not pat him or congratulate him; put your legs on to his sides, perhaps reinforced a little with a touch of the stick behind your leg, get him on the bridle and jump the fence again properly. If he does it well, then you can really make a fuss of him, but if he does not, take him round again, and again if necessary.

Punishments and Rewards

If things do go wrong, do not perpetually blame the horse. If you have spent hours schooling a horse and he has accepted that you are the boss, he does what he is told; if something then goes wrong, who is to blame?

Horse blamers are easier for a trainer to correct than the riders who constantly blame themselves. It is sometimes difficult for a trainer to give such people the courage and the confidence to do things more positively. One possible way of doing this is to take the decision making away from them: the trainer tells them what to do and if things go wrong, they can blame the trainer for it. They can then work more purposefully because they know that half the responsibility is on the trainer's shoulders. In fact, because the riders then attack more, they often get what they are riding for, and have no one to blame – the perfect situation.

When a fence has been jumped badly or in an awkward style because the horse did not respond to your legs, do not reward him and say 'well done, at least we got over the jump'; move the horse briskly forward with your legs, (perhaps reinforced with a smack behind your leg with the stick), on the bridle, and without hurrying make a more purposeful approach next time round. This will most often give you a good jump for which you can reward your horse.

Remember that the stick is not always a punishment. The stick is to reassure the horse that you are with him, and it will satisfy him that you are purposeful and mean what you say. He will gain confidence from that and give you less trouble in the future.

Confident horses are those whose riders never allow them to become confused, and a horse can be confused as much from rewards as from punishments. If you reward and fuss over your horse when things are done correctly, *never* reward him when a mistake has been made – whether the mistake was yours or his. If you reward a horse after a mistake, he will never be able to tell the difference between right and wrong.

Whatever you are working on, always strive to finish on a good note. If you are having trouble at a fence, and it is the end of the session, lower the jump so that your horse can put in a really good one at the finish. Never allow yourself or your horse to end on a sour note, and try to leave the school happy with your day's work.

Jumping Corrections

To correct any jumping fault, always look for the opposite condition. For example, if a horse tends to rush, he is probably listening to you only when he is going slowly. Unfortunately, very often, the opposite to the problem is not immediately apparent.

Often, more can be achieved on the landing side of a fence than on the take-off side. The anticipation of the landing will condition a horse's approach to a fence; if you change his landing, you change his approach.

Rushing

Start a rushing horse over a very small, vertical fence and turn him in to face the jump only about two strides away from it; this avoids giving him 20 or 30 metres in which to get excited on the way in. Once this horse has jumped the fence, bring him to a halt as quickly as possible, but not too violently. This exercise is best done with a fence situated so that it can be jumped from both directions. Continue to jump the horse from both sides, by straightening up two strides out and stopping immediately after the jump. As the horse becomes used to the routine, increase the time he has in which to look at the fence before jumping it. If he starts to anticipate the halt, make a few changes – sometimes halt completely and other times proceed at the trot.

If, when you give him more time to see the jump, he goes back to rushing, return to the shorter approach until you find that you can be straight, with a sensible trot dictated by you, for as long as you like. If you are satisfied, then is the time to try again in canter.

Horses should enjoy jumping, but they should not jump only because they enjoy it. They jump because they are going at a speed and in a direction dictated by the rider, when a fence gets in their way. They jump because they know what is required of them. If the horse jumps only for enjoyment, he can just as readily refuse; he must jump whenever you demand that he should. If he enjoys the work, that is a bonus.

Running Out

Some people think that horses who run out are horses who do not care to jump. This is not so; run-outs are not refusals, they are changes of direction, which, along with pace, should be dictated by the rider. If your horse runs out, be more positive. Keep a good contact with both reins, give him plenty of leg and keep riding him until he is actually in the air. Never appear to ask him whether he is going to jump; rather, let your attitude be that he will jump and you will follow. If the horse then stops in front of the fence, and you are confident that he could have jumped it, then you can give him a firm reminder that you are the boss. If he runs out, keep your whip ready on his run-out side, as a reinforcement to the already strong leg aid you are giving.

Always be positive. If you put your leg on to go from walk to trot, it is not good enough for the trot to begin two strides after you have made the signal. The aim is to get an instantaneous response to the signals, no matter what it is that you are trying to achieve. When you see a good stride, you have no time to think about aiming for it; seeing a stride is an instinctive flash, as should be your horse's response to your signals. Legs on must mean 'go on *now*'; anything less is not enough.

3 Related Distances

So far you have worked in the field or in the school, and have set your jumps and grids to suit the peculiarities of your horse; in short, you have made it easy for yourself. Now it is time to start thinking about taking your horse away from the comfort and security of home, and making a journey into the uncharted waters of the show ring, where the course designer will set his distances without bearing the stride of your horse in mind. He will use related distances. These are great for the horse who has exactly the average stride and who takes off and lands in exactly the right place every time.

In fact, such a horse probably does not exist. All horses occasionally stand off a little or get too close, and this affects the striding between the landing and the next element. What the course designer has measured out as three strides could easily become three and a half for you, so your job now is to develop methods of overcoming these little crises in competition.

Related distances are introduced into showjumping courses to test the rider as much as to test the horse. If your horse is not quite normal in his length of stride, it will not matter too much in a combination with one non-jumping stride: if he is short, he will be 30-45cm too far off and if he is long he will be 30-45cm too close; he will have to be just a little quicker in front to get out. Neither of these problems should worry you very much.

If, however, you extend the distance between the jumping elements to three non-jumping canter strides, you ob-

viously multiply the striding problem by three. At the end of a related distance of three or four strides, the error in your approach to the second element will be that much more acute.

The Horse's Work

Poles on the Ground

Uses Perhaps the best way to start coming to terms with related distances is to work with a pole, and later poles, on the ground between fences. This is an ideal exercise for correcting various problems: it lengthens short-striding horses, shortens long-striding ones and brings the horse down if his head and shoulders are too high. Some horses have a habit of making the highest part of their jump beyond the highest part of the fence. If your horse is doing this, he probably consistently knocks down rails with his back legs. Bear in mind that the horse's hind quarters cannot go up until his head and shoulders start to come down, and he needs to be taught to come down at the back of a fence, so that his hind quarters can easily follow through.

Ground poles are also good for teaching horses to cope with ditches and broken ground lines generally. There is now an increasing number of permanent showgrounds in Great Britain and more and more permanent fences, of which the Devil's Dyke at Hickstead is perhaps the best known. In fact the Devil's Dyke is rather like a cross-country 'coffin' fence.

The ground slopes away on the landing side of the first element, there is a ditch at the bottom and an uphill take-off for the jump out. If a horse is encouraged to approach the first element of such a combination with his head low, he will automatically be on his forehand and you, the rider, will undoubtedly be in front of the movement. From such a position the horse is bound either to refuse or to have the rail down.

Putting a pole on the landing side of jumps during training ensures that the horse brings his head down after the jump. The pole, in effect, simulates a ditch and the horse will naturally lower to look at it, which is no bad thing as long as you stay with the movement. The pole

will also help short- and long-striding horses overcome their particular difficulties and will lead, eventually, to mastering the inherent problems of related distances.

Combinations The following combinations will provide a progressive sequence of jumps.

1. To start working with ground poles, put a trotting pole on the take-off side of a small vertical fence. The pole should be about 2.75m in front of a 60cm jump and the horse should be presented at this until he is trotting in quietly, stepping over the pole and popping over the little jump. When the horse is coping well and is

Fig 57   A pole on the ground approximately 2.75m in front of a small jump. The horse steps over the pole in trot and the next stride is over the jump.

69

loosened up, put a ground rail on the landing side of the jump about 3.5m away. This will give him a step over a pole, a little jump and a canter stride over the pole on the ground. As the horse sees the ground pole on landing he will lower his head. You must anticipate this and concentrate on maintaining rhythm and following the movement throughout the jump.

2. Once the first combination is established, add another jumping rail, a hole higher than the first jump, a further 2.75m from the canter stride pole on the ground. What you have now is a pole 2.75m from a 60cm upright, a pole on the ground 3.75m further on, and a 75cm upright 2.75m beyond that.

3. Consolidate the second line of jumps and then change the rein. Put a pole 2.75m in front of the 75cm jump, and move the other two ground poles in to the feet of the 60cm upright, which is now raised to 83cm so that it is slightly higher than the first jump. You are now on the other rein, and if you can comfortably step over the pole, pop over the first jump, make a non-jumping canter stride and jump out, you can raise both jumps one or two holes.

4. To change the look of the sequence for the horse, you can now put a cross pole under the upright rail coming out. This will merely fill in and change the look of the fence a little. When this last combination is comfortable, you can make a spread by putting another rail up behind it.

Naturally if your horse is very long

Fig 58   Here a pole is placed on the landing side too, about 3.5m from the small jump.

Fig 59   The rail on the ground is 2.75m in front of the first element.

Fig 60   The second rail on the ground is about 3.75m from the first small
jump and 2.75m before the second element.

Fig 61   The pole on the ground between the fences regulates the horse's canter stride between the fences.

Fig 62   The take-off for the second element.

Fig 63 Clearing the second element.

striding, you must extend the distances above a little to start with; if he is short striding, you will find that the pole on the ground will encourage him to stretch just that little bit more. He may even make a very small jump over the pole on the ground to bring him into the take-off zone for the next fence. If you think that the distances are still too long for your horse and your temptation is to shorten them, you should instead try raising the pole on the ground 5-10cm. This will make him stretch even more as he opens out over the pole and will put him more easily into the desired take-off zone. The pole on the ground will effectively have modified your horse's stride. On the other hand, the pole on the ground will discourage long-striding horses from making too big a jump over the first element which would leave him too close to jump the second properly.

What the ground pole is actually doing is acting as a broken ground line to the second fence and, as such, it is of great benefit to horses who have trouble with ground lines in the show ring. Many horses do not like viaduct walls and ditches simply because they present a broken ground line. Working with ground poles can, with patience, teach them that there is really nothing to worry about.

You are now beginning to modify the stride and to reassure the horse that he should not be frightened of fences like Devil's Dyke. You can also bring the horse down if necessary – that is, if he is the sort of horse who jumps so high in front that he has difficulty bringing down his forehand to allow his back end to clear the fence.

Everything you have done so far has been for the benefit of the horse; when the exercises on related distances are extended, however, you will begin to use them for your own benefit.

The Rider's Work

From your work at home, you will be aware, perhaps painfully aware, of your horse's striding problems. Now it is time to come to terms with your own striding, so that you can accurately translate distances on the course to the natural striding pattern of your horse. Knowing the distances between elements will influence not just what you do between fences, but also how you approach the first element.

For instance, on a 15-metre distance between two jumps, if you take two canter strides you will be a long way off the second element, particularly if it is a spread; if you take four strides you will be asking the horse to climb his way out. Three strides is what is required, but these three strides can vary. You might approach the first element on a fairly normal stride only to find that the horse puts in a long one and you jump too far over the first element. Obviously the larger your jump, the closer you are going to land to the second element, and a really big jump will make your three canter strides into two and a half. You will be able to tell if this is happening as the horse makes the jump and it is at this stage that you have to decide what you are going to do about it. If you have made an enormous jump and left yourself only two and a half strides, your plan should be to stride after landing, make a half halt to produce a shortened stride, and then another full stride to give the horse the correct take-off position for the second element.

If, on the other hand, you make a poor first jump and land short, the distance between the obstacles will be longer than expected. Do not wait until you are faced with a huge stand off at the second before you think about what to do. As you jump you must make the decision to push on and lengthen all three of the strides, so that you leave the horse with a comfortable jump at the end.

Poles on the Ground

Combinations   Some further combinations of poles on the ground are useful at this stage:

1.   Instead of the second upright, add further canter stride poles. This means that the horse is faced with a trotting pole, a small jump, a ground pole 3.5m away (for the canter stride) and further ground poles, all 3.5m from each other, for him to tackle as he canters away from the jump. Ideally you can work up to four such poles so that you have a trotting pole, a jump and four non-jumping canter strides which are dictated by the poles on the ground. When the horse does this happily, you can reintroduce the second jump 2.75m away from the last canter pole.

Obviously you are going to need a considerable amount of room to do this exercise properly but it is well worth it if you can find the available space. If you cannot, two canter poles are better than nothing.

2.   As you progress, you can gradually raise the heights of the two jumps, and you should try to get into the habit of calling out the number of non-jumping canter strides that the horse makes. One of the most common mistakes is to call out 'one' as the horse's front feet touch the ground from the first jump. Landing is not a stride; you must be patient and not call 'one' until you are negotiating the first canter stride pole.

Fig 64   Poles placed on the ground between jumps can be used to work on related distances.

Fig 65   Having negotiated the small jump, the pole influences the first non-jumping stride.

Fig 66   With the aid of the poles, the rider can learn to assess the number of non-jumping strides required between elements.

Fig 67   Horse and rider arrive accurately in the take-off zone to clear the second element.

When you do this exercise, you will end up with a distance that is slightly shorter than is considered normal for four non-jumping strides. This is because you are approaching in trot (making the landing shorter), and the poles are dictating where the canter strides are made.

3. Once the exercise has reached the stage of jumps just over 1m high at each end, and the horse is easily making the canter strides dictated by the poles, the time has come to start taking out the canter poles one by one. When they have all been taken out, you should still be able to trot over the trotting pole, pop the 1m or so jump and make four even canter strides before jumping out. Ideally the horse will remember the conditioning of the poles, but he may be inclined to put in three long strides and one short, or four shorter strides with another very short one at the end. If he does this, reintroduce the poles and work through the exercises again.

4. As soon as the horse can do this, take him away and jump a single fence somewhere else. This is to clear his mind before extending the distance between the two related fences by a couple of metres and making the approach in canter. Do not allow yourself to be worried or intimidated by this change.

Approach the first fence as though it were a straightforward single fence and, as you jump, decide what you are going to have to do to make the required four canter strides to the second element. You may, of course, have to do nothing. If your horse makes a normal jump over the first, and is making normal working canter strides, you will simply have to sit there, with your legs close but not pushing, holding him between leg and hand in balance and rhythm. He will make his canter strides and do the jumping for you.

Naturally, you should never be doing *nothing* when riding. However, you should not pull and push the horse for the sake of pulling or pushing; if he is active, between leg and hand, and has impulsion, you must simply stay calm, keep the horse balanced, and the rest will look after itself.

Related distances are normally measured in multiples of 3.7m but you must learn to be flexible. With experience, you will find your own multiples as you learn about your horse's stride in any given situation, and as you learn whether the distance between any two jumps is going to be too long or too short for you and your horse. When you know what to expect in a given circumstance, you are in a position to act accordingly.

Walking the Course

Walking the course before any show-jumping competition is of crucial importance. Unless you walk it, and take notice of it, you will not have memorised it sufficiently to allow you to concentrate on your riding.

Walking the course is not simply an exercise to establish that fence 2 follows fence 1 and so on; what you are doing is measuring the distances in the doubles and combination fences. You need to know these because short or long distances influence the way in which you are going to approach particular fences and how you are going to tackle the space between them. Your jumping strides must all be precise.

Some people measure their distances from the middle of one fence to the middle of the next. Others measure from the inside of the back of the first fence to the front of the next. You can adopt either method as long as you know whether the distances are normal, long or short for you and your horse. If the distance is normal, you will approach the first element like a normal single fence. Having jumped it, keep the horse straight and, using your legs to maintain the rhythm, jump out the other end. If the distance is fairly short you must try not to jump in too far by keeping the approach a little more rounded. As you jump, follow the movement and, again, keep the horse straight without actually pushing him. Sit still and feel the benefit of your grid work as the horse folds up quickly for the second part.

Longer distances will require you to make a big, bold jump over the first and to ride with purpose, using more leg to help the horse cope with the combination.

Distances, however, are not all you should concentrate on when you walk the course. Look carefully at the state of the going and decide which studs you are going to use, if any. Note any undulations in the ground, as your tactics for downhill and uphill approaches will be different. Remember, too, to have a look at the jump-off course. The quickest horses do not always win classes; the win is often due to the rider who has seen the shortest route.

The more care you take while walking the course, the less trouble you will have when you jump, so walk it alone, and do not stop to chat to other riders unless you are talking to someone who's opinion you respect. A more experienced rider can give you useful advice. Try to memorise all relevant information which will increase your chances of achieving that aimed-for clear round.

4 Approaching Advanced Jumping

As your showjumping career progresses, you will meet dozens of different types of fences and each will demand your respect. There are many different ways of jumping familiar fences, as well as special fences – particularly water and ditches – which frequently make novice and intermediate riders take fright.

Jumping Diagonally

There will frequently be times when you wish to jump a fence diagonally. You may want to save time in a jump-off; whatever your reason, the fundamental thing to remember is to maintain your line of approach throughout the jump. You must land on the same line as that from which you took off, just as you would if you were making a straight approach to the jump. The only difference here is that the fence is angled underneath you as you jump.

Practice

The obvious danger of being on an angle to the jump is that the horse can more easily run out. Alternatively, if you surprise him with the unusual approach, he may well knock the jump down so, to familiarise your horse and your eye with the new circumstances, you must first practise on a smaller scale.

Start with a 45-60cm rail, placed so that it can be jumped comfortably from both directions, and approach it in trot from directly in front. Concentrate on aiming the horse straight at the middle of the fence and, as he loosens up, gradually start to approach from a slight angle. One of the most common mistakes when teaching a horse to jump on an angle is to ask him to jump with too much of an angle at the first attempt. Introduce him to the idea of an angle a few degrees at a time, and stay on the line of whatever angle you have chosen as you jump through on the other side.

Eventually you will build up your own, and the horse's confidence, and you will be able to approach from 45 degrees to the jump without the horse attempting to run out in either direction. Naturally this requires that you ride with purpose and continue to do so until the horse is up in the air.

When you think you are both comfortably coping with 45 degrees in trot, you can raise the jump a little, narrow the angle again and approach in canter. The principle is exactly the same as in trot. Look at the centre of the fence, jump straight across the middle and leave on the same line as the approach.

If the horse lands with the correct leading leg, maintain the canter and make a big circle to approach the jump from the side you have just left, and from the opposite angle. Do not worry too much about moving your weight to influence

Fig 68   A small fence is used to practise jumping on the angle.

Fig 69   Clearing the jump, the horse maintains the line on which he approached.

the leading leg on the landing side; too many riders almost jump off the horse in their attempts to make him change legs while in the air. However, if your horse is balanced, you will frequently find that looking in the direction in which you wish to go will be sufficient for him to land on the correct leading leg. For example, if you approach in canter at 45 degrees, with the horse in off foreleg leading canter, look resolutely left as he jumps the fence, not before; he will then usually be in near foreleg leading canter on the landing side.

Now you can raise the jump again and make a large figure of eight, with the fence at the centre of the figure. Stay in canter, unless you are on the wrong leg, in which case trot and change, and continue riding the figure eight until you are happy jumping from both angles on both sides. Eventually you should have little difficulty jumping a fence diagonally in a jump-off, and landing on the leading leg you need for the next jump.

Correcting Problems

Unfortunately, as in most exercises of this kind, you will probably discover that the horse finds the jump easier from one direction than from the other. He may even be inclined to run out to one side or the other. If, for example, he is inclined to run out to the left, you might think that it would be better to approach the fence from the right, so that the horse has more fence to look at. The fact is, however, that if you approach from the right, you are encouraging the horse to run out to the left; if you come from the right and he moves towards the centre, he is already going from right to left and it is easier for him to convert this movement into a full run-out.

Horses inclined to run out left should approach from left to right towards the centre of the jump; you will then find he is less inclined to attempt a run-out. However, do bear in mind the fact that run-outs are *not* refusals, they are simply changes of direction which are the responsibility of you, the rider.

Those of you who compete in cross country as well as showjumping will find this exercise useful when it comes to jumping corner fences: when you come to an angle of two rails, the best thing to do is to imagine a line that bisects the 'V' of the angle, and then jump straight over that imaginary pole. Obviously the real poles of the corner will be at angles to you, but if you jump for the imaginary pole and stay on your line through the jump, you will give yourself every chance of jumping clear.

Ditches and Water Jumps

The advent of permanent showgrounds has given rise to permanent fences – banks, water jumps, water ditches, dry ditches and many others – and course designers seem to be aiming to create a more 'natural' type of fence at their shows. Some actually construct water jumps, but many use water trays in an attempt to simulate ditches on their courses.

What you must bear in mind when you come across such fences is that, in most cases, the jump itself is not altered; the only difference is that it now has a broken ground line, and the tray of water under the jump alters its overall appearance.

If your horse is used to jumping ditches or things on the ground under fences he should not pay too much attention to the water tray; the tray has more effect on the rider than on the horse, since if a horse cannot judge the depth of a ditch or a water jump, it should not inhibit him or change his attitude to the jump at all. Starting a horse over such fences early in his career, should prevent him from being bothered when he encounters them in the show ring. Horses who have been introduced to water jumps and ditches when they were young tend to accept them as an integral part of their jumping lives.

Practice

To help train a horse for such jumps in your home field you do not necessarily need to dig a ditch or build a water tray – you could simply put a plank on the ground underneath a small rail, or you could put down a row of sacks (paper sacks should have a plank over them to prevent them from flapping around). Alternatively, a sheet of polythene or even a couple of horse blankets will work just as well; it does not matter what materials are used as long as they change the appearance of the jump and create a broken ground line.

Whatever you use, it should make absolutely no difference to where you take off and where you land, although your horse might make a slightly bigger jump than usual. Younger horses, of course, are likely to lower their heads to take a look at the obstacle without, hopefully, inhibiting their forward movement.

At the start, keep the jump small, at least until the horse realises that he will come to no harm from the ditch, or materials you have substituted. Soon he will accept the situation and you can help

him by not looking down yourself. You should keep your eyes on the highest part of the jump, not the lowest part of the ditch. If you do this, the depth of the ditch should not matter, either to you or to your horse.

Initially the jump should be small enough for the horse to walk up to it, warily perhaps, and still hop over it when he has decided there is no danger. Only when he has been reassured can you start to raise the height. Eventually you will be able to ride at the fence with purpose, going straight and forward, and with the horse looking only at the jump and not at what is underneath it. He will realise that the fence does not necessarily require a different technique, even though it looks different.

Proper water jumps are slightly different in that the horse has to cover more ground – 3-4m of water, or almost 5m in an international arena. Sadly too many riders think that they have got to gallop flat out, in order to open out the horse's stride sufficiently to clear the distance. These people should remember that the normal canter stride of a horse covers around 3.5-4m, so the horse does not need to be galloping when he reaches the water; indeed, they are more likely to be wrong at the fence if they approach in a long, flat stride.

Ideally you will approach the fence in a good working canter, and in the style in which you wish him to jump. It might be helpful to fix your gaze on the line where the brush in front of the water joins the ground. This is because you should get as close to this line as possible if the distance is to be cleared; however it is no good reaching this line on a short last stride. A good, lengthening canter stride is what is required, so that the horse can make

Fig 70 As an introduction to water trays and jumps a plank is placed under a small jump, causing the horse to look down.

Fig 71 The lowered head is not a problem as long as the horse does not lose momentum.

maximum use of his own abilities in jumping the obstacle.

When starting a young horse over water jumps, have a low pole over the water. In fact, some shows will do this if the water is in a novice class. This is to teach the horse that although he needs to be gaining ground forward, he also needs some height to be able to go clear. Horses with a flat approach tend to dive and land in the water or on the tape.

Ideally, then, you should be approaching the water in working canter, lengthening the stride without it becoming too long and flat. If you feel that you must open the stride out marginally, you may, as long as you can maintain the rhythm and ride the horse right up to the brush in

front of the water. This is as important here as when you are jumping a triple bar; if you stand off a stride, the highest point of the horse's jump will be too early and you will come down too soon.

The secret of all these jumps – water jumps, water trays, ditches and similar obstacles – is not to panic. They look different, certainly, but take the time to think about them logically. A water tray makes no difference to the height of a jump; a one-metre ditch under a one-metre fence does not make a two-metre jump. A one-metre ditch with a rail over, is simply an ordinary jump, as long as you do not let your horse, or yourself, look down into the ditch.

Fig 72 A small parallel fence is made to look different by a pole placed on top.

Banks

If you are approaching a bank, and have to jump up on to the obstacle, your approach will be exactly the same as it would be for a one-metre vertical fence. The fact that the horse lands on higher ground will not matter if your approach is balanced and even. Stay calm and the horse will understand the situation, and react accordingly.

The sooner you introduce your horse to these 'natural' jumps the better, and he will more readily accept them as a normal part of his life. Portable water jumps and water trays can turn up in any competition and you must be ready for them. You will see people at local shows in a panic because there is a water obstacle that they had not expected. If you are one of these people, it would pay you to throw a rug under a fence in the practice area so that if your horse is going to look down, he does so outside the ring and not inside it. If, however, you ring the changes at home and attempt some variations in practice, neither you nor your horse will be surprised by anything the course designer introduces. The little traps that are set will have less and less effect on your final results.

Fig 73 Coming off a tennis court type bank with a rail behind. The rider is looking for the next fence.

Fig 74 *The beginning of a varied sequence, which starts with a small upright fence.*

Fig 75 *A small spread fence is the second element.*

Fig 76 A filler is added to a small spread.

Fig 77 Finally there is a larger spread and filler.

The Jump-off

Jump-off tracks obviously vary considerably, and not all will suit you and your horse. Some will require tight turns, others will be more open and will demand a short gallop to make up time. However, if you have jumped a clear round in the first phase of the competition, having taken the trouble to 'read' the course and make the correct distancing and studding decisions, it is unwise to gallop flat out against the clock. Clear rounds win classes, so your best bet is to keep up the good work by jumping a double clear.

In the early days of your competitive career, you should treat the jump-off in exactly the same way as you treated your first round: calm, balanced, unhurried and aiming to be clear. Later, when you have more experience, you can start cutting the corners by taking a slightly shorter route. Naturally the temperament of the horse will play a large part in your progress in jump-offs; if he is excitable, and it has taken a long time to settle him, it is obviously unwise to aim for more than another quiet clear round. If, on the other hand, he is a little lazy, it will probably do no harm to race against the clock.

Remember, however, that the fastest horse does not always win. Very often the winner is a slower horse whose rider has worked out a quicker route. This is where your hours of schooling on the flat will be invaluable. You will be able to take a shorter line simply by taking one or two straight strides before a fence, or by jumping diagonally. (Note, however, that diagonal jumping is best reserved for uprights; jumping diagonally over spreads can be very risky.) Indeed, if you are in a position to utilise all your flat work exercises at will (flying changes, for example), you are in a very good position to jump fast and clear.

Try to think of the jump-off as an extension of the first round. Ideally you will approach the last fence at the same pace as the first and, in between, you will have made a series of lengthening and shortening strides which put you in the right place for each jump and got you through the finish with all rails intact. Consistent speed is important because it allows you to settle the horse into a rhythm while enabling you to think about the striding you have chosen for your quicker route.

Approach to Competition

Everyone in the equestrian world has a level at which they compete and the obstacles in the next level of competition will almost certainly appear daunting. Bear in mind, however, that horses eligible for Newcomers (Novice) can be at different stages of their training. A horse new to Newcomers, who has not won any affiliated money, is in a different league from one who has almost won enough to be ineligible for Newcomers.

You must recognise that the level at which you are working is a level worth working at. Be happy that you are at that level, and jumping in that class, and if you do have the odd upset learn to treat it philosophically. What seems like a disaster on the day of a competition can, three weeks later, seem to be merely a minor setback on the road to your goals. Accept a few minor problems with grace, and do not let them influence you into changing your working pattern dramatically.

There is nothing worse than repeatedly gaining four faults. Remember that four faults are largely a matter of luck – or bad luck. One day you may rattle a fence and it will stay up, another day you may barely touch it and it will clatter to the ground. It is, of course, frustrating to have one down, but if you can learn to accept the mistake within the context of the whole course, you will realise that four faults are not the end of the world. The day will come when you will be lucky, jump a clear round and be on your way.

If you are making important mistakes every time you go out, you must rethink the situation and perhaps go back a stage to consolidate. If, however, you are progressing satisfactorily, you should be thinking about the future. If you are about to progress to a new class (from Newcomers to Foxhunter, for example), jump a course at the higher level before you are actually compelled to jump in the bigger class. While you are still qualified for your present class you have the option, so have a go at a friendly-looking course before you are promoted – better to choose an introduction at your own convenience than wait until you have no choice left.

Finally, if you have a problem and you find that you cannot resolve it on your own, seek professional advice.

5 Lungeing

If you are short of time, lungeing is a very good way of both schooling the horse and exercising him. Half an hour on the lunge will benefit him much more than half an hour hacking on the roads. However, you must recognise the difference between lungeing for exercise and lungeing to teach him and to make him work that little bit harder.

Basic Approach

Equipment

Rider The most basic requirement is to wear gloves when you lunge. The horse can pull the lunge rein through your hands very fast and it can inflict some nasty burns: gloves will help to avoid, but will not entirely eliminate the possibility of this. Do not wear spurs when you lunge. If you do happen to get caught up and fall over, the spurs will be of no benefit to you and may cause you an injury. These precautions are simply a matter of being sensible and minimising the risks.

Horse Providing your horse is not too strong or unpredictable, do not think that you cannot lunge because you do not possess a cavesson headcollar (cavesson halter/head stall). It is perfectly acceptable to lunge from the bit and there are various methods especially designed for doing just that. One such method is to connect the lunge line to the opposite bit ring, pass it over the horse's head, and thread it again through the inside bit ring. In effect this means that the lunge is acting on the opposite side of the head to that from which you are lungeing; if you are lungeing to the left, on the left rein, the lunge line will be fastened on the right side of the horse's mouth, passed over his head behind his ears, and threaded through the left bit ring. Alternatively you can pass the line directly behind the chin (rather than over the head) and through the left bit ring before bringing it back to the hand. It is not a good idea to have the line connected to the side of the mouth from which you are lungeing. If you do, and the horse pulls, you may pull the bit through his mouth, causing him some pain and encouraging him to think up some evasions.

Rider's Position

It is common sense – although, surprisingly, this is not seen by some riders – to lunge the horse from a position in line with the hind quarters. This will give the feeling, both to you and the horse, that you are driving him along from behind. Remember, too, that to gain any lasting benefit from lungeing, you must be able to ask him to perform perfect circles, which means that you must stand on one spot. If you walk about while you are lungeing, the horse will make ovals and other odd shapes.

Try to pivot on your inside foot, that is, the foot on the side to which you are lungeing. If you are lungeing to the right,

Fig 78   The chambon encourages a long low outline. The horse is relaxed.

pivot on the right foot while keeping the contact with the lunge line as near as possible to the contact you would have with the reins. There should not be a sag in the middle of the lunge line. If there is, the horse is not connected to you at all and he is doing what he wants to do, not what you tell him to do. Similarly, he must not move outwards on the lunge line so that he pulls you off your pivoting foot and unbalances you.

Obviously there are no rigid rules when dealing with horses. If the horse turns in on you when you are lungeing, you have no choice but to move; to stay still in one spot would mean losing all

contact. Ideally you should be thinking a little quicker than the horse. At the first sign that he is about to turn in, you should take a step towards the hind quarters – lungeing to the right you would take a sharp step to the left to get in behind him again – which is the only position from which you can keep him moving forward.

Aids

At a basic level, lungeing is simply an extension of the voice and whip aids the horse was given when he was first broken. In the beginning he was given the command 'walk on' and the command was followed up with the whip coming in behind to give him a little encouragement. The technique is the same on the lunge; lightly use the whip until he willingly obeys your voice command only. The same method applies for the transition from walk to trot. At first, tell him to trot and follow it up with the whip until the time comes when he associates the word 'trot' with the transition.

If the horse does not respond to the voice for downward transitions and the halt, take a step in the direction in which he is moving. That is, if you are on the left rein, step to the left so that you are in line with his head. This prevents him from feeling that you are driving him on and discourages him from going forward.

Horses who have been properly broken will probably respond to the voice quite readily, but if it is some time since he has been lunged, you may have to remind him of the commands that you are going to use. Sometimes, of course, different words were used when the horse was broken but, in the main, it is not the words but the manner in which you say them that is important. For upward transitions, the voice is brisk and compelling and for downward transitions the words are slowly drawn out. You want the horse to associate the type of voice you use with the type of movement you require. You will be surprised how quickly horses do associate these ideas.

Transitions

When you start, the horse should walk quietly away from you; he should not scatter away, buck or try to play around. To encourage him to walk away, gently push his head and, if you want him to go on the right rein, step quietly to the left. This places you near his hind quarters and behind his head, and has the effect of urging him forward.

Always ask him to walk first and never let him go into a trot immediately. The horse should be aware of being under some discipline and starting him off in the walk allows you to get him used to voice aids before you urge him up to trot. If he is very fit and well, do not ask him to walk for too long as he is likely to become bored and will look for mischief. You can allow him to canter a circle or two to let off steam, but most lunge work is best done at the trot – you can dictate the pace more easily and the horse will understand more readily that he is doing what you want rather than what he wants.

In downward transitions from trot to walk and from walk to halt, the horse should be attentive and obedient. Insist, for instance, that he halts on the circle, so that *you* can walk up to *him*. The practice of shortening the lunge line while the horse works, to get him to stop, encourages bad habits. He has plenty of opportunities to learn these habits, turning in on the lunge, for example, without needing extra help from you. If you establish that he must stop on the circle, he will be less inclined to turn in and you will have won an important victory.

This is rider psychology at work, and it is not to be underrated. You may be working with a young horse who has not really come to terms with voice aids. If he breaks into a trot of his own accord when he reaches the extent of the lunge line, give the command 'trot' anyway. You are not making him trot, but you are planting the seed of the idea in his mind and he will eventually associate the word with the movement.

Similarly, if the horse is trotting along quite perfectly, there is no point in bringing him back to the walk too soon, as there is every chance he will disobey you. Let him keep trotting around quietly until his own inclination makes him slow (all horses have a point on the circle where their trot is not quite as active). When he is just about at the slowing spot, give the voice aid to come back to the walk. If he breaks into a walk of his own accord before you give the command, say 'walk' anyway and, as with the trot, he will gradually remember the association.

This method of persuading the horse to do what you want is far more effective than spending minutes telling him to walk when he has no intention of doing so. This is a waste of time and it teaches him to disobey the voice aids. Do remember, however, that whatever you do, you are unlikely to be able to make him walk if you are standing at his hind quarters. If you take a step in front of the movement it will help him to slow down.

Lunge Circle

Try to make sure that the horse has room to do what you want. The lunge circle should be at least 15 metres but, if you have a long enough lunge line, 20 metres is even better. You make it easier for yourself if the horse is comfortable in his circle, with his back legs following the tracks that his front legs have made. If the circle is too small, the hind quarters will tend to swing outwards and he will be performing a variation on shoulder-in in the circle, which is not what you are aiming for.

Lungeing with the chambon and side reins is discussed in Chapter 8; suffice to say here that some horses are at risk of losing their balance on the lunge, and you should give them all the protection you can: brushing (interfering) boots front and rear should always be used, and overreach (bell) boots are essential for jumping.

Lunge Jumping

Whether you are lungeing straight off the lunge line, using a chambon or using side reins, the horse will be benefiting. Most horses seem to enjoy the experience – notice their prancing and bucking when they first start to canter – and they also seem to enjoy it when you use a jump in the lunge circle. Naturally, the more responsive the horse is to your voice, the easier it will be to school him over a lunge jump, so if you plan to jump him, establish the pattern on the flat first. Let him hear and get used to the voice commands before you introduce the jump.

It can be a very beneficial exercise to jump a horse with no weight on his back but, if you have little experience of controlling a horse in lunge jumping, do not be too ambitious at first. Keep it simple and start with just a single little rail, with perhaps a rail on the ground just in front as a take-off marker. Eventually you will be able to be a little more ambitious and ask the horse to jump more complicated fences but, during the early days, be cautious. Concentrate on keeping yourself in control. Do not let the lunge line wrap itself around you or the horse's legs and, whatever you do, do not wrap the lunge line around your hand. Just keep it looped up neatly so that you can let out a loop easily if you want the horse to lunge a bigger circle (or avoid

Fig 79   A simple fence over which to lunge.

injury if your horse begins to scatter). If you wrap it around your hand you can do yourself a nasty injury and cause unnecessary problems for the horse.

Safety

For lunge jumping, it is best to use an enclosed area or, at the very least, the corner of a field, so that you have two sides to keep him contained. Start with a tiny upright post on the inside of the jump (obviously a large wing would get tangled with the line) and run a pole from the top of the upright to the ground in the direction of the horse's movement. This acts as a guide for the line and minimises the possibilities of disaster.

Common sense would tell most people, but not all, that if you are working in a field, you should place your jump facing in towards the corner. You do not want to give the horse a whole open field

to look at, as soon as he has made his jump. Make sure, too, that the wall, fence or hedge which you are using is large enough to prevent him from jumping out at the other side, as a double. *Never* attempt to jump on the lunge with the horse wearing a chambon or side reins.

Generally speaking, providing you are sensible and do all you can to minimise the risks, you will get as much benefit from lunge exercises as the horse. It is good for you to see for yourself the outline that the horse makes and, particularly, to see what he does with his legs when he jumps. It will show you, perhaps better than any other method, why you must adopt certain riding techniques when you are on his back.

Remember, above all, do not start lunge jumping until everything is going smoothly on the flat. Do not try to run before you can walk.

Fig 80   Allow sufficient line to run up the guide rail.

Fig 81   Start small. You can make the jump larger as you become more proficient.

Method

Set up your jump before you start and establish the lunge circle so that the horse is trotting easily, but inside the line of the jump. He should be trotting calmly inside the jump, without fretting. If he is quiet enough, move yourself so that you are in line with the fence and, if this does not unsettle him, take two steps sideways as he trots away from the inside of the jump, so that when he comes around the next time he is facing the centre of the fence. The angled pole will guide the lunge line over the inside rail support and the horse, all being well, will easily pop over the little fence. He will probably land in a canter and you will have to walk with him for a stride or two, which will take you away from the fence, in order to slow him down. This means that he must bypass the jump again on the next circle so that you can reposition yourself for him to be in the right line to jump. As you continue, you will find that, by following a pace or two every time he jumps, the period of time between jumping the fence and coming back to a calm, relaxed trot will lessen, and he will begin to accept the lesson as an integral part of his everyday work. When that happens it is time to change the rein, change the lunge line guard rail, and work from the other direction.

If he is working well over the small upright, you might raise it a hole or two and put a ground rail about 3m in front of it. This gives him something to look at and to step over, and stops him from becoming too confident and blasé, while encouraging him to retain sufficient impulsion to work properly.

Finally, always take your lunge line with you whenever you go to a show. Even if you reap no other benefit from the exercise, it will often be useful at the showground when you unload an excited horse from the box (van or truck). As soon as you unload him take him off to the quietest corner you can find and lunge him for ten to twenty minutes so that he has a chance to settle before being asked to work amongst the other horses. Lungeing like this can sometimes calm a horse down more quickly than any other method, and it loosens and warms his muscles without the added burden of weight on his back.

6 At the Show

For most people who compete horses, the routine of the day of the show is permanently etched on to their minds. However, many riders often seem more nervous than their horses on competition day and, in their anxiety, are often forgetful. A brief survey of the most important points to remember is appropriate.

Travelling

Not everyone's circumstances are the same. Some riders will be lucky enough to be able to leave everything to a groom, but most of us have to do everything for ourselves. More often than not this means getting up a couple of hours earlier to feed, groom, plait (braid) the mane and make everything ready for the show. Hopefully you will have packed the horse-box (van or truck) the night before to reduce, if not eliminate, your last minute panic about what you might have forgotten. Doing things the night before means you can take things easier in the morning and this helps to prevent your horse from becoming over-excited.

Once you have fed the horse – he should have finished eating at least an hour before being boxed, and at least two hours before competing – groomed and plaited him, you should still have time in hand to prepare him for travelling (trucking). You may use bandages (wraps) or travelling boots, poll (head) guards, knee and hock boots (protectors), tail bandages and tail guards; the

list is endless. All these things take time to deal with and you will only add to your own panic, and perhaps excite your horse, if you start to run out of time.

Naturally you should allow time for actual loading, especially if your horse has shown a reluctance to load in the past. In addition, allow extra time for travelling if your horse is young or an anxious traveller.

It is also essential that you know your route to the show before you leave the field. You will only add to any anxieties and worries that you have already if you spend time on the journey wondering which turning to take. It can all be avoided with just a few minutes of advance preparation.

On Arrival

When you finally arrive at the showground, try to park on flat ground and, if it is a hot day, try to be near a tree or whatever shade is available. Unload the horse, check that he has travelled well and then find out at what time your classes are, what ring they are in, and other details. Also find out if the classes go in drawn order, or whether you have to put your number down. If you must put your number down, consider whether you want to ride early or late. Naturally you will probably have to ride fairly early in the class if you are riding more than one horse, which usually means working in before walking the course.

97

Working in

Try to keep your warming up procedures as close to normal as possible. Make the horse loose and attentive to your signals and work in quietly over a small fence to establish your pattern. This early fence need not be too big but the last couple of fences before you actually go into the ring should be about the height of the competition fences. The very last practice fence should be an upright, again of about competition height.

The important consideration when practising is to make sure that you do not leave too long a gap between the last practice jump and your entry into the ring. It is useless to warm the horse up and make him ready to go, and then to find that there are ten horses before you. When this happens, the tendency is to sit around talking to other waiting riders and then to wonder why the horse has the first fence down through lack of impulsion.

Fig 82   A shade far off the planks.

In the Ring

Once you are in the ring, establish your pattern. You have plenty of time to do this and getting your working canter going is crucial. Even after the bell has gone you have 45 seconds before you must go through the start, so take your time and make sure everything is going well before you commit yourself.

During the round, always keep a picture of the next jump in your mind and avoid the temptation to look round if you rattle a fence. Nothing is worse than looking round to see if you have knocked down the last fence, only to have the next one down because you were not properly prepared.

Bear in mind, too, that it is the fences that are important – just because there is, perhaps, a large crowd around the ring does not mean the jumps are any higher. On average you will only be in the ring for 90 seconds – not too long to concentrate, so do everything you can to forget the crowd and keep your mind fully on

Fig 83   Hickstead rails. The front legs a little too close for comfort.

Fig 84 The Hickstead bank – its less steep side, as used in the Derby Trial. The horse here is a little impetuous.

the job.

At the end of the round you might be feeling the elation of a clear round, the frustration of four faults or the gloom of a disaster but, whatever the circumstances, you must try to come out of the ring as calmly as possible. It is very difficult not to get a little angry if things have gone wrong and some horses would make anyone want to swear, but you must try to remain fairly unperturbed. Never allow yourself to become churlish about your mistakes. Not only is it disagreeable for the spectators to see you pulling your horse about in anger, but you could also undo weeks of work that you have patiently built up in training.

It is natural to have a post-mortem after a round but try not to allow it to go on for too long. No matter who made the mistake, you or the horse, you both live on to fight another day. Mistakes in the ring have to be corrected at home, calmly and dispassionately. You are unlikely to be able to develop your horse into one who jumps consistent clear rounds unless you first learn to control yourself.

After Competing

After one round you may well have a long wait before the next class and you should do all you can to make the horse as

Fig 85   The triple bar in a novice class at Hickstead.

Fig 86 A spread fence at the Horse of the Year Show, Wembley.

comfortable as possible. If the wait is a couple of hours he can have a small drink (not a bucketful, though) and, if your first class is at about 9 a.m. and your next class not until 4 p.m. you can give him a small feed. The tack should be removed, sweat marks and saddle marks brushed off and, depending on the weather, he should be covered with an appropriate rug (blanket or sheet).

At the end of the day it is important to be as systematic as you were when preparing to leave the yard in the morning. Remember to remove the horse's studs (a common omission) and prepare a haynet

(hay bag) so that he can have a snack on the way home. You can have one, too – there is nothing wrong with stopping for a take-away as you travel, but there are few things worse than leaving a horse loaded up while you have a meal in a restaurant. It is a kindness to the horse to keep him in the horse-box only as long as is necessary.

When you arrive home again check him over for cuts, lumps and bruises and, if the ground at the competition was very hard, it might be a good idea to leave stable bandages on overnight. Feed and water him as normal and, if you can, check him again later at night. Horses who have been competing may become thirstier than usual and you may find an empty bucket when you arrive for your last check.

Finally, on the morning after the show, check him over again thoroughly for swellings, heat, cuts and other problems, and trot him up to make absolutely sure that he is sound and hearty after his day out.

7 Bits and Bitting

Bits are a very complicated subject and to write fully on them would require a complete book. You only have to consider the plethora of variations on the simple snaffle or bridoon to see why. Loose ring snaffle, eggbut snaffle, straight bar, twisted, gag, Fulmer, vulcanite, rubber, long cheeked – the list goes on and on. Many riders are understandably confused and bewildered when they come to the subject of bitting. The common questions are: what difference does the bit make, and what is the best bit for my horse?

Choosing a Suitable Bit

A bit is not so much a device put in the horse's mouth, as one put in the hands of the rider; no matter what bit you put in the animal's mouth it is only as severe as your hands make it.

Controlling the Horse

The first requirement in any successful horse and rider combination is that the horse is under control. For this reason, a bit with perhaps a curb chain may be preferable in some circumstances to the much kinder snaffle, if the rider then has to saw, yank and tug at the horse's mouth in order to get any kind of signal through. No rider can succeed unless he can control the pace and the direction of the horse so, if necessary, a slightly more severe bit, used correctly and with kindness, is much

better than fighting the horse in a battle of wills.

Schooling or training at home is a much calmer and more controlled environment than that of the show ring. It will be much easier for you to achieve control working in your back field than it will on a competition day and you should bear this in mind in your bitting. You can manage proceedings at home to suit yourself but the situation is very different from competition when the adrenalin is flowing. For training, therefore, keep the bit in the horse's mouth as kind and as soft as possible. Your horse may work for you at home in an eggbut snaffle, but once you are in the competition arena you might need something a little stronger or a little more severe to get your message across.

It will be a matter of trial and error, but when you do find the bit that works best for you in the ring – a bit that gives you the control to jump a strange course of fences – keep it solely for that purpose and never use it during training sessions at home. The stronger bit should remain part of your armoury for imposing your will over his excitement on the day of competition. This is especially important if your horse is inclined to look for evasions and ways around the bit at home. Looking for a way out with a snaffle is very different from doing it with a Pelham, for example. The more severe bit will force him to concentrate when his instinct is simply to charge off and have a good time.

Bit Types

Over the years I have discovered one or two little points about bits which may be of help as you pick your way through the maze of bits available. A Pelham seems to encourage a horse to lower his head and to keep it down whereas a gag snaffle does the opposite – it is likely to raise the head. Bear in mind, too, that the effect of any bit will vary slightly according to the shape of the horse's mouth – what works for one horse will not necessarily work for another. Many riders will find a particular bit which suits their style of riding, and most horses will go kindly for them.

Curbs You may decide that you need a bit with a curb chain to get what you want from the horse. But which of the curb chain options do you choose? A Pelham would, with the effect of its roundings, give you a curb (Weymouth) while using only one rein, and you may prefer this. Others favour a simple double (full) bridle with two reins in each hand – this, however, requires some skill as, in novice hands, the reins can become knotted up. Some prefer the straight ported bar and curb of the Kimblewick. All have their advantages and all work for some horses. You will have to try, gently and with patience, to discover what works for you. My own preference for a

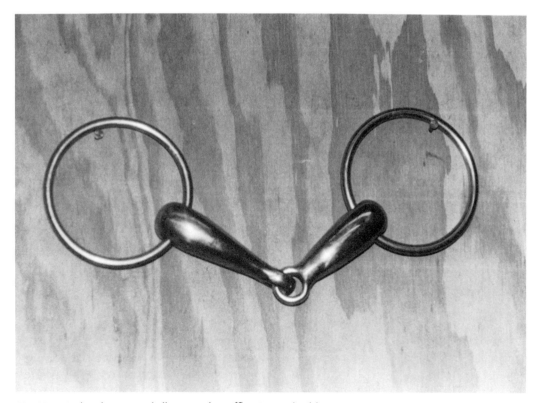

Fig 87   A plain loose ring, hollow mouth snaffle. A very kind bit.

curb chain is a simple double bridle, but normally only for use in the show ring – I would only very rarely use one for training and schooling sessions.

Other options A long cheeked snaffle, which is derived from the Tennessee Walking Horse bit is another possible option. The longer cheek pieces on this bit work rather like a gag on the poll as well as on the corners and the bars of the horse's mouth. With proper use, this allows extra leverage to help keep the horse's head down.

Remember that nosebands and martingales can alter the influence or effect of a bit quite markedly. Cavesson, drop, cross-over, flash and Kineton nosebands, along with the effect of the running martingale, can all affect the severity of a bit. For instance, the martingale is to prevent the horse's head from coming up too high, not to keep his head down, so if you lengthen or shorten the martingale by just a couple of holes the effect on the horse's mouth can be dramatic.

Bitting Problems

Many riders say that their horses' mouths are so light that they have to ride them in

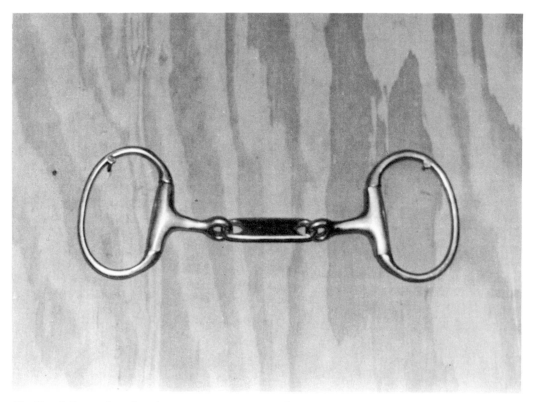

Fig 88 A Doctor Bristol, with two joints, can suit some horses. It is thinner than the normal snaffle, which makes it that much sharper.

rubber snaffles and can barely touch their mouths with the reins. In fact their horses do not have light mouths, their mouths are totally unresponsive.

For a horse to have a 'mouth' you ought to be able to feel in your hands the energy that you have created with your legs, and you should be able to push the horse between leg and hand to create impulsion. The horse is then pushed into the bridle with the mouth accepting the bit. If you cannot do this, and you are having trouble with the horse's mouth generally, look in his mouth, as well as at your riding, for the solution. Are his teeth too sharp? Does the bit fit cor-rectly? Is it too high and pinching his mouth or too low and banging his teeth?

Fitting

To fit correctly, a bit should lie neatly at the corners of the mouth and the skin at the corners should make one fold or wrinkle as the bit exerts a gentle upward pressure. It should not be so narrow that it squeezes the mouth with the side pieces, or so wide that it bangs around from side to side. If the bit that you are using is wrong, it is better to borrow alternative ones rather than buying them – you will probably have to try several

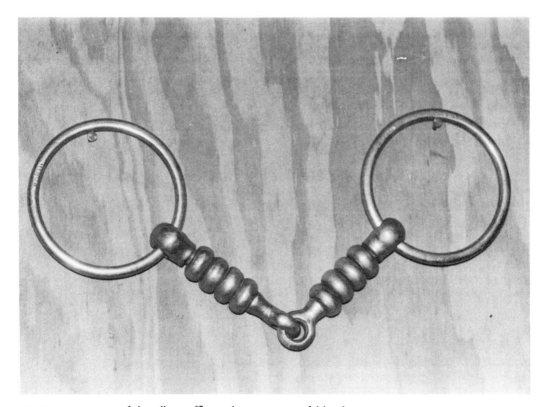

Fig 89   A variation of the roller snaffle – a bit requiring tactful hands.

before you find your ideal arrangement.

Dry Mouth

Another reason for horses' problems coping with their bits is 'dry mouth'. Indeed, it is not hard to imagine the irritation and pain that metal rubbing against dry skin will cause in a horse's mouth. Every movement on the bit is agony and he does everything he can to evade your instructions.

If your horse has this problem, he must be made to salivate. A mint, a lump of sugar, even just a handful of grass may help to start the saliva glands in the mouth working. This is necessary because a horse must be relaxed and flexed at the poll, and have relaxed muscles behind the saddle before the saliva glands can begin full operation. Anything that you can do to start them off can only help the horse. Should your horse have a particularly dry mouth it may pay to try a key (player toggle) ring snaffle. This might encourage him to mouth the bit a little – although not too much, which is as bad as too little movement – but you must ensure that he salivates so that he can have the necessary lubrication for the bit to move against his skin without painful irritation.

Tongue Over the Bit

Yet another bitting evasion occurs when the horse puts his tongue over the bit. This can start as an evasion against the hand being too hard, or caused by the bit being too low in the horse's mouth but, whatever the reason, once he learns to draw his tongue back over the bit you have problems. When the tongue is on top, the bit is acting directly against the bars of the mouth without the cushioning effect of the tongue. The metal of the bit will bang on to the sensitive bars and the horse will look for every possible evasion, little realising that his tongue over the top of the bit is the cause of all his troubles.

Obviously to avoid this you must ensure that the bit is not too low in the mouth. A horse can move his tongue over a low bit without really wanting to. You could also use a cavesson noseband. A thick cavesson, done up quite tight, will stop the horse from opening his mouth too much and will give him less room to manoeuvre his tongue inside the mouth. If all fails, however, you will have to consider the use of a tongue guard or tongue port. This will physically prevent the horse from drawing back his tongue and moving it over the top. The metal tongue guard is probably most suitable: this is a thin piece of metal with a port in the middle (and probably a bar across the port) that fits just into the corners of the horse's mouth. It is on its own strap and you simply fit it over the bit you are using. Once in place the horse cannot draw his tongue back. There are other tongue guards – a rubber one, for instance, actually fits over the centre of a snaffle – but they are not particularly effective. The metal one will give best results.

If your horse is working with his tongue lolling out of the side of his mouth you should check that the bit is not underneath. A protruding tongue is often a sign of this, although not always. Some horses let their tongues loll out of the side of their mouths even when the bit is in the correct place. This would be penalised in a dressage test but is of no consequence to a jumping horse. The problem only arises when the tongue is out because it is over the bit.

The Bitless Bridle

No word on bits would be complete without mention of the bitless bridle. There are two variations of such bridles but the most common, and the one most widely known, is the hackamore. It is a common misconception that hackamores are gentle bridles. Far from it – a hackamore exerts great leverage with its long cheek pieces which are connected to the noseband. The effect of this is that the horse is ridden virtually on the front of his nose, and not on the bars of the mouth, as with a normal bit.

There is, however, a place for the hackamore, and indeed there may be nothing else to use if the horse you are riding has a chronically sore mouth. A hackamore will give you much more control when it comes to pulling up a horse who is, perhaps, very strong on the bit; the disadvantage is that it is not so easy to control the horse's direction.

The hackamore was made very popular by the great Eddie Macken when he was riding Boomerang. For various reasons, Eddie chose to use a hackamore on Boomerang and this lead hundreds of young hopefuls out to buy hackamores for their horses. Invariably this was a mistake. A hackamore in the hands of a master can be a great boon but it can be damaging when used by people with considerably less skill than the top riders.

Bitless bridles, perhaps even more than bitted ones, need to be expertly fitted. During the time when they were fashionable, far too many people fitted them too low, purely out of ignorance. The disastrous effect of this is that the horse's nose is blocked and he cannot get air through to his lungs. Pulling against the hackamore then causes him to gasp for air.

Even if fitted correctly hackamores can cause a lump on the horse's nose, through the great leverage exerted by the bridle. They are only to be used with the utmost respect and novice and intermediate riders should, if at all possible, avoid them and leave them for the experts.

Conclusions

The horse should respect the rider's hands without being frightened of them. He must be comfortably under the rider's control and he must be under that control whether he is at home or in the show arena. This is not always an easy thing to achieve. Some very good riders, through no fault of their own, have horses who are very strong in the mouth, especially in the ring. Usually the horse has got used to one particular bit, even a fairly harsh one, and has learned either to evade it or to catch hold of it so that the rider has problems in competition. Invariably the answer to this problem is to have four or five bits, all different, and to interchange them when the horse is competing – even to the extent of changing a bit between the first round and the jump-off. This keeps the horse guessing and he does not have time to work out the evasions possible with one bit before he is confronted with another one. This approach may be the answer to your problems, if you have a very excitable horse.

One final word on bitting in general: some riders follow a practice of making a small cut or slit in the corners of a horse's mouth to force him to be more responsive to the hand. Apart from the unforgivable cruelty of this practice, the practicality is that when the wound heals over, the scar tissue will be thicker than ordinary skin and the mouth will be even less sensitive than it was before the wound was made. If you know of anyone who has been thinking of using this barbarous technique, stop them immediately.

8 The Use and Abuse of Gadgets

At present it seems there are more gadgets for sale in riding shops than ever before; everyone seems to have something that can turn the novice into an expert overnight. There is a place for most of these gadgets in riding, but they should be seen simply as the means to an end, not an end in themselves. No one should use gadgets out of habit or without considering whether they are deriving any benefit from them. For example, many riders, even top show-jumpers, are inclined to use draw reins and running reins as a matter of course and this sells their riding ability short. Good riders can put their horses' heads wherever they want, without the use of draw reins, but they still go on using them as a matter of habit.

There is an adage in the equestrian world generally that: 'only experts are capable of using draw reins and experts won't use them'. This is off the mark, as many 'expert' riders do use them – but to what effect? The problem is that as soon as the public at large sees a top name using draw reins, they all want to use them as well, whether they have the ability or not. They see good horses going in draw reins and they think all their riding problems have been solved in a flash. In reality they simply cause further problems for themselves and end up with a horse even more delinquent than before.

There are, of course, a few aids that are more than simple convenient gadgets:

lungeing in a chambon, for instance, can be very useful in that the chambon, correctly fitted, exerts gentle pressure on to the horse's poll and encourages him to lower his head. The only reservation is that the chambon is used *only* while lungeing, never while riding the horse, when it can be very dangerous. Side reins qualify for the same proviso. They are good as an encouragement to the horse to lower his head (as opposed to forcing his head down) and they help him to work in a contact on the lunge, rather than trotting around aimlessly and sloppily.

Draw Reins

Used properly, of course, draw reins and running reins can fulfil similar functions. The draw rein comes from the girth between the front legs and the running rein from under the saddle flaps. A horse that is inclined to hollow his back and throw his head into the air may benefit from draw reins. They can help him to start rounding his outline and they may, used sympathetically, produce the desired result quicker than any other method. However, you should not consider them to be a short cut. You can use them to point a horse in the right direction but, once the seed is sown, you must return to more traditional schooling so that the horse understands why he is required to do all the strange things he is asked.

To get the best from a draw rein you should have the rein coming from between the front legs, through the bit and into the hands and the draw rein should be about 5cm shorter than the direct rein. If you do this, when you ride the horse forward into the bridle, he will feel the pressure on the bars at the corners of his mouth and he will drop his head. As he does so he puts himself back on to the direct rein, and the draw rein does not affect him in any way until he tries to raise his head again.

The horse will soon realise, using this method, that lowering his head is something of a reward and he will accept the outline imposed by the direct rein as that which you, the rider, require. Should he raise his head, the draw rein will exert slightly more pressure and the head will come down again. You will be surprised how quickly he learns that when you push him up to the contact he should relax his lower jaw, lower his head and flex at the poll. There is nothing like the reward of pressure eased to encourage him in to an obedient response.

If, on the other hand, you maintain draw rein pressure all the time the horse will never experience the reward of relief. Even if he lowers his head, the pressure will remain and you will be encouraging him to push upwards in an attempt to rid himself of your constraints. The practical effect is that as soon as you remove the draw rein, his head will shoot straight up because that is what the horse has been trying to do while wearing the draw rein. The whole purpose of the rein will have

Fig 90   Use of the draw rein – here the draw rein is active.

Fig 91   As the horse lowers his head, the draw rein loosens.

Fig 92   The horse is now on a direct rein.

113

been defeated.

Normally the draw rein runs from the girth, between the horse's front legs, up through the bit and back to the rider's hands, but this is not the only fitting. The reins can also be used over the top of the horse's head, down through the side of the cheeks, through the bit and back to the rider's hands. Using this method, the further back you bring the rein down the horse's neck, towards your own body, the more leverage effect you have with it. Start with the rein just in front of the withers and, as soon as the horse gets the idea and relaxes his head, push it forward until you have it just behind his ears.

Some horses respond to this method more readily than to the more common use of the rein but the method is irrelevant; what matters is that the horse is taught that relaxing the poll and the lower jaw, and rounding the outline, is rewarded by less pressure and discomfort. In short, draw reins used correctly can help a horse and, from this point of view, there can be little against them. Do beware, however, as they can easily become a rod for your own back.

Fig 93   Without the draw reins . . .

Fig 94   In fact, the horse can still be flexed.

Market Harborough

If you are having trouble with a horse who tosses his head in the air, a Market Harborough might be preferable to draw reins. For horses who are hollow and above the bit, the Market Harborough has very much the same effect as the draw rein: you push the horse up into a contact and, ideally, lower his head at the same time. Certainly the Market Harborough can give you a little more control in keeping the horse between leg and hand when it comes to jumping a course of fences.

However, the Market Harborough is again only a means to an end, never the end in itself. You do not always want to have to ride the horse in a Market Harborough. It should be used only to educate the horse. Start with it quite tight and gradually loosen it off until the day comes when it is not required at all.

Balancing Rein

The balancing rein can be a useful gadget, but, like the draw reins and Market Harboroughs, they have to be applied with common sense and humanity. A horse who is already on his forehand, perhaps with his neck sticking straight out from his withers, should never be required to work in these devices. Obviously such a horse does not benefit at all from a riding aid that requires him to come down even lower in front. Balancing reins exert tremendous leverage, and an additional pulley system can exert even more, on to the bars of the horse's mouth. If your horse carries his head very high, perhaps in a haughty, peacock fashion, there may be a case for the use of balancing reins but only in the company of someone who understands the science of them and loves horses. Without these two attributes, even the most well-meaning rider can do lasting damage.

Side Reins

To begin with, side reins should be about 2-5cm shorter than a length which would allow the horse to carry his head in a normal standing or trotting position without side reins. They should be the same length, despite the common habit of shortening the inside rein in an attempt to encourage bend. Inside rein shortening causes the horse to swing his quarters out. Even in lungeing you should consider the horse to be between the inside leg and the outside hand. Obviously the side reins can never be an adequate substitute for the rider's hands but, if they are the same length, the horse can get the idea, with his power coming from the hind quarters and the person doing the lungeing pushing him forward into a contact with the voice. This allows the horse to relax the jaw, flex at the poll and adopt the desired working outline.

Martingales

The most common martingales in use are the running martingale and the standing martingale, although the Irish martingale, which is normally used in racing, does sometimes occur in a showjumping arena; it is simply a short strap with a ring at each end that is designed to keep a rein at each side of the horse's neck. Although it is unlikely that you will come across the Irish, you will undoubtedly use the running or standing martingale often. Unfortunately both are frequently mis-used – particularly the standing mar-tingale.

Standing martingales are not allowed internationally but, when used correctly, they are useful for preventing the horse's head from going above a certain height. This is of benefit, particularly to horses that habitually carry their heads high. Horses such as those will have difficulty clearing their hind quarters over a fence – they will be faulting frequently – but, with a standing martingale, they will be encouraged to drop their heads on the landing side, so allowing the back end to

rise and clear the height. This happens because the standing martingale allows the rider's reins to go direct to the horse's mouth.

This is not the case with the running martingale, although it too will not inter-fere with the reins going to the mouth unless the horse raises his head above a predetermined level. Sadly many people set their running martingales too short because they think this will keep the horse's head down. This simply creates evasions. When a running martingale is too short, it produces a pulley effect; the reins go down to the ring and then upwards again to the mouth. This not

Fig 95   *Head up, with running reins in action, and the direct rein slack.*

only puts more pressure on the mouth, it also delays the signals you are giving the horse with your hands. If the running martingale is fitted properly, on the other hand, it will have no effect on the horse as long as he is going correctly. The extra pressure that the martingale brings to bear does not start to take effect until the horse begins to raise his head too high. Then it will have a steadying action with the reward of no pressure being given as soon as the horse adopts the outline required.

Whips and Crops

Although they do not fall into the category of 'gadgets', whips and crops are certainly the objects of frequent misuse and deserve a section to themselves. Always remember that the stick you carry is only to supplement the leg aid – it is not a headmaster's cane. A blatantly naughty horse may be given a crack every now and again, and, done correctly and at the right time, such action can save you time and trouble in the future. However, avoid the temptation to think of the whip as a punishing device; rather, think of it as a bit of extra leg muscle.

Fig 96   Head lowered, with the direct rein in contact and the running rein eased.

If you want to go from walk to trot you would close both legs on the horse's sides. Should nothing happen, you give the horse the benefit of the doubt and try again, with a touch more purpose. If, again, nothing happens you apply the leg strongly and, at the same time, or a split second later, use the whip to give the horse a smack behind the leg. This is simply an encouragement and a reminder to the horse that the next time you put your leg on you want him to go forward. It is, after all, much better to impose your discipline and control at the walk to trot level than when you are approaching a big parallel fence and find the horse is not going off the leg as he should.

Judicious use of the crop or schooling whip can, indeed often does, lighten the horse to the aids. It teaches him to go away from the pressure of the leg, and this means that you never have to apply an unacceptably excessive leg aid. If you use your whip properly you will never need to cave in the poor animal's ribs. You will simply give a slightly quicker leg aid and, if that does not work, apply leg and whip together. This should be a very civilised procedure.

What you will need to do, however, is to learn to use the whip in both hands. Practise changing it over from right to left, and vice versa, and use it, from time to time on the opposite side from normal. You can get used to this in your flat work training by always having your whip in the inside hand. If you can change your whip as automatically as you change your diagonal, the battle is almost won.

Spurs

Spurs, perhaps the most abused artificial aid in riding, are also a simple supplementary aid. They are to encourage the horse to respond quickly to the leg, for both forward and lateral movements. Unless they are used and fitted correctly, however, they can be implements of torture.

To be fitted correctly, the spur should lie just on the join where the boot hinges naturally with ankle movement. In this position you should be able to close your leg on the horse's sides with the spur not touching at all, because all the leg pressure comes from the calf, not the spur joint. If the horse responds to this leg pressure, so much the better, but if he refuses the aid, add a little lower leg pressure so that the spur contacts his sides.

When using spurs it is imperative to make sure that your legs are in the correct position, with the toes to the front. If you have your feet at right angles to the horse's sides, you can inflict injury with the spurs. Used properly the spurs should merely lie on the animal's sides and exert their influence with a very slight backwards movement of the leg. *Never* use spurs as if they were nails.

9 Horse Fitness and Welfare

Feeding

Quantity

Some people believe that the art of feeding a horse is to stuff him with as much as he can possibly eat – the more energy he takes in, the more energy he will have to give them. In fact, the prudent rider is the one who gives his horse just enough food for the job he is required to do. That rider keeps a weather eye on the horse, monitors his progress and has him looking, and feeling, a million pounds without him necessarily being overfed and excitable. The good feeder will know when the horse is going off his food before the animal does, and he will know how to tempt the horse back – providing, of course, that the loss of appetite was purely mental and not caused by illness.

This is not to say that horses should go underfed – far from it – but it is true to say that overfed and underworked horses cause more problems than they warrant. It is so easy to get it right, too, with just a little care. Modern foodstuff bags have an analysis of the contents printed on the outside so that you can work out how many calories, or 'working units' you are giving him. Naturally, what you do feed will be governed by the horse's size, conformation, breeding, age, the work he is doing and by any number of other factors. If you are in any doubt about how much food the horse should be getting, you will find that most reputable companies will be happy to send a nutritionist to your yard to advise on balanced feeding programmes. If you do keep your horse well fed, well housed, well shod and regularly wormed and rasped, you have the right to ask for a fair day's work. The measure of that is the progress you make with your daily training exercises.

Fitness

Obviously if you have the horse too fit for the job he is to do, you make things much more difficult for yourself, sometimes miserably so. A horse jumping Newcomers does not have to be anywhere near as fit as a *puissance* horse or one jumping Grand Prix courses. In essence, what you need is a horse who, when he has done the tasks or the competition you have set him, feels as though he has earned a rest – this is easier for both you and the horse. If he is so overflowing with energy that he wants to continue, he will become frustrated and cantankerous when not allowed to do so; you will then be in a desperate state by the end of a day spent trying to tend to your coiled spring of a horse. If your horse is of this type, get advice on diet immediately – it may radically change your riding life for the better.

Bear in mind, too, that the more work you give a horse the fitter he becomes. It is just as wrong to train too much as to overfeed. Young and novice horses are far better trained for two half-hour sessions in a day than one full hour; ideally the first half hour could be athletic schooling and the second half hour quiet hacking. The horse will be relaxed by the change of scenery, and a little canter, perhaps in some woods, will be a tonic for you and him alike.

By the same token, do not train your horse for an hour a day and keep him stuck in a stable for the other 23. If at all possible give him time at grass – at least two hours a day. He is, after all, a grazing animal. It is what he was born for, but there is a benefit in it for you as well. The simple act of bending to graze while in a peaceful frame of mind relaxes his neck and shoulder muscles. It is the horse's equivalent of a massage. If you do not have a field available for grazing, at least walk him out and graze him in hand for half an hour or so.

Hay

In addition to his daily graze, make sure you give your horse good quality hay. Many people boast that they have managed to get hold of a hundred bales or so of cheap hay and, when you inspect it, you find it is dusty and musty rubbish that gives every horse in the yard coughing fits. Good hay is an absolute necessity. It allows you to cut down a little on the hard food because it contains nutrients as well as roughage and it pacifies the horse. He will be happy to occupy some of the inactive hours of his day nuzzling and dreaming into his haynet. It is also good for you to hear the horse munching away contentedly in his stable, as you then know that he is in fairly good spirits.

General Welfare

The horse who is below par is no less a problem than the too fit horse. There is nothing worse than beating a horse for being lazy, only to find later that he was anaemic or generally unwell. The answer is for you to keep a tender and watchful eye on him. Blood tests are now readily available and, if your normally lively horse is lethargic and uninterested, you should ask your vet to perform one.

However, slightly less than peak performance may simply indicate that the horse needs a holiday. Jumping horses in work do a lot for their living and they expend physical and mental energy in abundance. Normally most horses seem happy to give their all, but all horses from time to time need to recharge their batteries.

In the old days, the hunter was put out for the summer and the jumper for the winter. This made sense and was economic. Now, however, showjumping is a year-round occupation so we can be more flexible about when we give the horse time off. Two or three months' rest during the year can be spread over two or three periods of a month each. This means that you can pick times to suit you and the horse and it also means that the horse does not become as unfit during each break as he would if he was out for longer.

Finally, in terms of general stable management, you obviously lessen the chances of infection and illness in the yard if you keep everything clean. Do not, for example, keep topping water buckets up. Clean them out regularly and fill them up with fresh water. Cleaning feeding bowls should be as automatic as cleaning tack.

Tack should not simply be cleaned to make it last longer. It will, of course, but the cleaning ritual is also an inspection. Check for old sweaty bits that are going to rub the horse's skin and for the odd stitch that might have come undone on the leather work. Better to get it repaired when there is just a stitch or two frayed than to have everything come apart when you are in the ring.

To sum up, the welfare of your horse depends, to a large extent, on the good habits that you develop in yourself. If you take care and do things properly the horse is much more likely to be good humoured and good natured – and he will obviously be much better equipped to do the work that you ask of him.

Conversions

Centimetres	Inches
1	$\frac{2}{5}$
2	$\frac{4}{5}$
3	$1\frac{1}{5}$
4	$1\frac{3}{5}$
5	2
10	4
20	8
30	12
40	16
50	20
60	24
70	$27\frac{1}{2}$
80	$31\frac{1}{2}$
90	$35\frac{1}{2}$
100	39

To convert centimetres to inches, divide by 2.54

Metres	Feet and Inches
1	3ft 3in
1.5	4ft 11in
2	6ft 7in
2.5	8ft 2in
3	9ft 10in
3.5	11ft 4in
4	13ft 1in
4.5	14ft 9in
5	16ft 5in
6	19ft 8in
7	22ft 11in
7.5	24ft 7in
10	32ft 10in
15	49ft 3in
20	65ft 7in

To convert metres to inches, multiply by 39.37

Useful Addresses

Great Britain

British Horse Society
British Equestrian Centre
Stoneleigh
Kenilworth
Warwickshire

The British Show Jumping Association
can also be contacted at the address
opposite.

USA General Information

American Horse Council
1700 K Street NW
Washington, DC 20006

Publishes an annual US Horse Industry
Directory which includes a full listing of
US equestrian organisations.

USA Young Adult

National 4 H Council
7100 Connecticut Avenue
Chevy Chase, MD 20815

US Pony Clubs, Inc.
329 South High Street
West Chester, PA 19382

USA Sport and Show Organisations

American Driving Society
P.O. Box 1852
Lakeville, CT 06039

American Horse Show Association
598 Madison Avenue
New York, NY 10022

United States Combined Training
   Association Inc.
292 Bridge Street
South Hamilton MA 01982

United States Dressage Federation Inc.
P.O. Box 80668
Lincoln, NE 68501

Further Reading

The Athletic Horse
Carol Foster

Educating Horses from Birth to Riding
Peter Jones

Dressage: An Approach to Competition
Kate Hamilton

A Festival of Dressage
Jane Kidd

Equine Injury and Therapy
Mary Bromiley

The Equine Veterinary Manual
Tony Pavord and Rod Fisher

Foaling: Brood Mare and Foal Management
Ron and Val Males

Guide to Riding and Horse Care
Elaine Knox-Thompson and Suzanne
  Dickens

The Complete Book of Horse Care
Tim Hawcroft, B.V.Sc. (Hons)
  M.A.C.V. Sc.

Horses are made to be Horses
Franz Mairinger

Long Distance Riding
Marcy Drummond

Pasture Management for Horses and Ponies
Gillian McCarthy

*The Performance Horse: Management, Care
  and Training*
Sarah Pilliner

The Complete Book of Ponies
Lorna Howlett

Riding Class
British Horse Society

The Systems of the Horse
Jeremy Houghton Brown and
  Vincent Powell-Smith

The Young Horse
Elaine Knox-Thompson and
  Suzanne Dickens

Index

Ability 7, 8, 9, 12, 20, 44, 47, 84, 111
Above the bit 27, 28, 115
Accepting the bit 107
Activity 14, 25, 34, 39, 40
Adjustments 16
Age of horse 8, 119
Aids (means of communication) 10, 14,
    15, 22, 23, 25, 28, 30, 31, 34, 37,
    45, 62, 67, 91, 92, 93, 111, 115, 117,
    118
Aims 7, 8, 10, 11, 12, 15, 23, 67, 78,
    88, 93
Anaemic 120
Angle
    flatwork 21, 22, 23
    jumping diagonally 31, 47, 79, 80, 81, 88
    pole 96
Approach 7, 10, 25, 31, 40, 45, 53, 58,
    59, 61, 62, 63, 64, 66, 67, 68, 69, 74,
    77, 78, 79, 80, 81, 82, 84, 85, 88, 109, 118
Assessing horse and rider 9
Assessing progress 9
Assessing strides 76
Athlete 26
Athletic 7, 9, 31

Balance 13, 20, 25, 26, 31, 33, 36, 44, 53, 58,
    59, 60, 62, 63, 64, 65, 77, 81, 85, 93
Balancing rein 115
Bandages 97, 102
Banks 81, 84
Bars of the mouth 108, 109, 115
Bascule 52, 63
Behind the bit 26
Bitless bridle 109
Bits 30, 38, 64, 90, 104, 105, 106, 107, 108,
    109, 112, 114
Bitting problems 106
Blood tests 120
Bored horses 8
Bridle 65, 66, 107, 109, 112
Bridle path 18
Broken ground line 68, 73, 81, 82
Bruises 102
Brushing boots 93
Bucking 59

Calm activity 45, 53
Cavesson 90
Cavesson noseband 106, 108
Chambon 91, 93, 94, 111
Change of direction 17
Circles 15, 17, 18, 22, 23, 28, 31, 34, 37, 45,
    59, 79, 90, 92, 93, 96
Clear round 78, 88, 89, 101
Coffin 68
Combination fences 77, 78
Communication 8, 9
Competition 68, 77, 88, 97, 98, 104, 109, 119
Concentration 8, 99
Confidence 9, 44, 66
Conformation 12, 119
Contact 14, 18, 22, 25, 26, 28, 34, 44, 58, 91
Corrections 16
Correct seat 44
Coughing 120
Counter canter 20
Course designer 7, 62, 68, 81, 85
Course of fences 7, 12, 89, 104, 115
Crossed jaw 26
Crossed poles 43, 47, 50, 52, 70
Cross-over noseband 106
Curb chain 104, 105, 106
Cuts 102, 103

Demi-pirouette 34, 35, 36, 37
Derby Trial 100
Devil's Dyke 68, 73
Direct rein 112, 113, 116, 117
Discipline 7, 9, 28, 47, 49, 92, 118
Distances 39, 40, 44, 45, 47, 48, 53, 61, 74,
    77, 78
Disunited 31, 34
Ditches 68, 69, 73, 78, 84
Double bridle 105, 106
Doubles 77, 94
Draw reins 111, 112, 113, 114, 115
Dressage 7, 9, 20, 108
Dropped noseband 106
Dry ditch 81, 82
Dry mouth 108

Eggbut snaffle 104

Energy 24
Engagement 12, 21, 26, 28
Equipment 90
Evading the bit 8
Evasions 8, 20, 25, 26, 28, 59, 90, 104, 108, 109, 116
Excitable horse 15
Extra stride 64

Facilities 8
Faults 10, 89, 101
Feed 97, 102, 119
Feeding bowls 120
Filler 55, 56, 87
Flash noseband 106
Flexion 42
Flying change 30, 31, 32, 34, 88
Forehand 12, 20, 21, 26, 34, 35, 36, 37, 45, 65, 69, 73, 115
Foxhunter 89
Fulmer snaffle 104

Gadgets 109, 111, 117
Gag snaffle 104, 105
Gait 25
General routine 8
General stable management 120
Girth 17, 31, 34, 35, 37
Grand Prix 119
Grazing 26, 120
Gridwork (stride, bounce, ascending) 44, 45, 47, 48, 49, 50, 52, 53, 54, 55, 58, 59, 60, 61, 78
Groom 97
Ground/Flatwork 8, 10, 16, 31, 63
Ground line (take-off pole) 45, 49, 68, 69, 70, 73, 74, 96
Guide rail 94, 95, 96

Hackamore 109
Hacking 120
Half circle 16, 17, 18, 35, 36
Half halt 25, 61, 74
Half stride 25, 61, 63, 64, 65
Hay 120
Haynet 120
Headstrong 15
Heat 103
Hickstead 68, 99, 100, 101
Hind quarters 12, 14, 17, 18, 20, 23, 28, 34, 35, 36, 37, 59, 63, 68, 90, 91, 92, 93, 115, 116
Hocks 26, 34, 42, 44, 53

Hock boots 97
Holiday 120
Hollow back 25, 26, 30, 115
Horse box 96, 97, 102
Horse fitness and welfare 8, 119, 120
Hunter 120

Illness 120
Impulsion 12, 15, 20, 22, 23, 26, 30, 62, 77, 96, 98, 107
Instructor 89
In the ring 99
Irish martingale 115

Jumping arena 10
Jump off 34, 36, 37, 78, 88, 109

Key ring snaffle 108
Kimblewick 105
Kineton noseband 106
Knee 42
Knee boots 97

Landing 31, 45, 49, 53, 59, 66, 68, 69, 70, 74, 77, 79, 81, 82, 116
Lateral movement 118
Leg and hand 24, 26, 27, 28, 29, 30, 44, 58, 77, 107, 115
Leg yielding 18, 19, 20, 21, 26, 28, 30, 31, 36
Lengthened and shortened strides 7, 12, 14, 15, 23, 38, 53, 62, 65, 68, 73, 74, 82, 84, 88
Loading 97
Long cheeked snaffle 104
Loose rein 15, 26, 28, 44, 58
Loose ring snaffle 104
Lumps 102
Lunge jump 93, 94
Lunge line 90, 91, 93, 96
Lungeing 90, 91, 92, 93, 96, 111, 115

Market Harborough 115
Medium trot 14
Mouth 30, 58, 63, 104, 107, 110, 116, 117
Muscles 28, 38, 96

Natural fence 81, 85
Newcomers 88, 89, 119
Non jumping stride 46, 51, 53, 57, 70, 74, 75, 76, 77
Noseband 109
Novice class 84
Novice horse 30, 31, 111, 120
Nutrients 120

Nutritionist 119

Obstacle 85
One-sided 16, 23, 30
On the bit 26
Outline 8, 9, 13, 14, 21, 22, 23, 25, 26, 27, 28, 29, 30, 91, 94, 111, 112, 114, 115, 117
Over-bent 26, 29
Overreach boots 93

Pace 58
Parallel 43, 44, 53, 62, 118
Pattern of work 10
Pelham 104, 105
Period of suspension 34
Permanent fences 68, 81
Physical exercises 7
Physical problems 8
Plait 97
Plank 82, 83
Poll guard 97
Position (rider) 55, 59, 60
Pressure of the leg 17
Problems 10, 16, 108, 120
Protection 93
Protruding tongue 108
Puissance 61, 119
Pulley system 115

Refuse to jump 65, 67, 81
Rein back 30
Related distances 53, 68, 69, 73, 75, 77
Resistance 25
Reverse half volte 16, 18
Reward 66
Rhythm 12, 14, 15, 21, 22, 23, 25, 26, 31, 34, 36, 37, 38, 40, 44, 45, 53, 55, 58, 59, 61, 62, 63, 70, 77, 78, 84, 88
Riding systems 9, 16
Ring the changes 85
Rising trot 15, 43
Roughage 120
Routine 10
Rubber snaffle 104, 107
Rug 102
Running martingale 106, 115, 116, 117
Running reins 11, 116, 117
Run-out 67, 79, 81
Rushing 10

Safety 40, 94
Saliva glands 108
Schooling 10, 20, 26, 28, 36, 65, 88, 90, 104,

Schooling – contd.
106, 111, 120
Seeing a stride 61, 62, 64, 67
Short stride 10, 64, 65, 74
Shoulder-in 18, 20, 21, 22, 23, 24, 26, 30, 31, 36, 93
Show ground 97
Show ring 104, 106
Side reins 93, 94, 111, 115
Signals 8, 9, 14, 15, 18, 23, 25, 26, 31, 34, 36, 67, 98, 104, 117
Slower trot 12, 13
Snaffle 104, 106, 108
Soft side 16, 18, 21, 23
Sore mouth 109
Spectators 101
Speed 10, 12, 16, 24, 39, 40, 44, 59, 61, 62, 65, 67, 88
Spread 43, 44, 47, 53, 55, 56, 57, 58, 61, 64, 70, 74, 86, 87, 88, 102
Spurs 90, 118
Standing martingale 115, 116
Stand off 64, 65, 68, 74, 84
Stick/whip crop 65, 66, 67, 91, 92, 117, 118
Stiffness 16
Stiff side 16
Stirrup 55, 60
Stirrup leather 18, 23
Straight bar snaffle 104
Striding to a fence 25, 39, 44, 88
Studs 78, 102
Suppling exercise 21, 24, 26, 30, 31
Swellings 103

Tack 102, 121
Tail bandage 97
Tail guard 97
Take-off zone 63, 64, 65, 66, 73, 74, 76, 82
Technique
  jumping 7, 55, 63, 82
  lungeing 92
  riding 7, 9, 12, 34, 94
Teeth 8, 107
Temperament 9
Tennessee walking horse bit 106
Tongue guard 108
Tongue over the bit 108, 109
Trainers 9, 11, 39, 44, 65, 66
Training 7, 8, 9, 10, 11, 16, 30, 38, 59, 88, 101, 104, 106, 118
Transition 15, 16, 24, 25, 26, 31, 63, 92
Travelling boots 97
Triple bar 84, 101

Trotting poles 38, 40, 41, 42, 43, 45, 69, 74, 77
Turn on the forehand 16
Twisted snaffle 104

Ulcerated mouth 8

Variations 8, 11, 23, 24, 39, 45, 85, 104
Vertical fence (upright) 62, 69, 85, 86
Vet 120
Viaduct wall 73
Voice 91

Vulcanite snaffle 104

Walking the course 77, 78, 97
Warming up procedure 21, 45, 98
Water 102
Water jump 79, 81, 82, 84, 85
Water tray 81, 82, 83, 84, 85
Working canter 12, 24, 53, 62, 77, 82, 99
Working in 97, 98
Working trot 12, 13, 14, 15, 24, 38, 39, 45

Young horse 9, 26